HOPING for the BEST, PREPARING for the WORST

EVERYDAY LIFE IN UPPER CANADA, 1812–1814

HOPING for the BEST, PREPARING for the WORST

· ·

EVERYDAY LIFE IN
UPPER CANADA,
1812–1814

DOROTHY DUNCAN

DUNDURN
TORONTO

Editor: Michael Carroll
Design: Jennifer Scott
Printer: Webcom

Library and Archives Canada Cataloguing in Publication

Duncan, Dorothy
Hoping for the best, preparing for the worst : everyday life in Upper Canada, 1812-1814 / by Dorothy Duncan.

Includes index.
Also issued in electronic format.
ISBN 978-1-4597-0592-0

1. Ontario--Social life and customs--19th century. 2. Ontario--Social conditions--19th century. 3. Ontario--History--1791-1841. 4. Canada--History--War of 1812. I. Title.

FC3068.D85 2012   971.3'02   C2012-900151-1

1   2   3   4   5   16   15   14   13   12

We acknowledge the support of the Canada Council for the Arts and the Ontario Arts Council for our publishing program. We also acknowledge the financial support of the Government of Canada through the Canada Book Fund and Livres Canada Books, and the Government of Ontario through the Ontario Book Publishing Tax Credit and the Ontario Media Development Corporation.

Care has been taken to trace the ownership of copyright material used in this book. The author and the publisher welcome any information enabling them to rectify any references or credits in subsequent editions.

J. Kirk Howard, President

Printed and bound in Canada.
www.dundurn.com

Dundurn
3 Church Street, Suite 500
Toronto, Ontario, Canada
M5E 1M2

Gazelle Book Services Limited
White Cross Mills
High Town, Lancaster, England
LA1 4XS

Dundurn
2250 Military Road
Tonawanda, NY
U.S.A. 14150

In memory of
Gordon Fuller Duncan
who served in the
Royal Canadian Air Force
in the Second World War
and all the other
men and women who have
defended Canada over the centuries.

CONTENTS

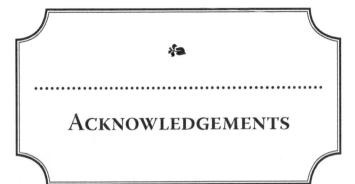

ACKNOWLEDGEMENTS

I WANT TO express my sincere appreciation to all those individuals, members of organizations, and staff of the institutions who contributed to this book with words of encouragement and support, suggestions, proofreading, and clues for further investigation.

First of all a very special thanks to those dedicated individuals who ensured that this publication emerged in a timely manner: Colin Agnew for his research, constant support, advice, and sense of humour — I couldn't have done it without you; and the staff of Dundurn Press for their expertise, knowledge, and patience, particularly Kirk Howard, Michael Carroll, Jane and Barry Penhale, and Jennifer Scott.

Among those who made invaluable contributions are: Jane Beecroft, Oshawa; Dr. Carl Benn, Ryerson University; Valerie Buckie, Curator, Park House Museum, Amherstburg; June Chambers, Tecumseth and West Gwillimbury Historical Society; Janet Cobban, Curator, John R. Park Homestead Conservation Area; Lynne

Campbell and Kathryn Harvey, Guelph McLaughlin Archives, University of Guelph; Paul Delaney, Tiny, Ontario; Madelyn DellaValle, Curator, Windsor's Community Museum; Pat Fillion, Black Creek Pioneer Village, Toronto; Kathy Fisher and Pauline Pennett, Ermatinger Clerque National Historic Site, Sault Ste. Marie; Dr. Rae Fleming, Argyle, Ontario; Emily Gibson, Toronto; Debra Honor, Amherstburg; Jeanne Hopkins, Willowdale; Joyce Horner, Town of Markham; Jeanne Hughes, Richmond Hill; Edward Janiszewski, Toronto; Ruth Keene, Niagara Falls; Linda Kelly, Sheguiandah, Manitoulin Island; Carolyn King, Mississaugas of the New Credit First Nation; Kenneth Kidd, Features Writer, *Toronto Star*; Rosemary Kovac and Mya Sangster, Fort York National Historic Site; Robert Leverty, The Ontario Historical Society; John MacLeod, Fort Malden National Historic Site; Judith McGonigal, Sault Ste. Marie; Brian Narhi, St. Catharines; Lori Nelson and Lisa Moncrief, Lake of the Woods Museum, Kenora; Janice Nickerson, Upper Canada Genealogy, Toronto; Michael Nickerson, Toronto; David O'Hara, Administrator, Fort York National Historic Site; Stephen Otto, Friends of Fort York and Garrison Common; Dennis Pollock, Beaverton, Ontario; Joyce Pettigrew, Otterville, Ontario; Douglas Robinson, Chatham-Kent, Ontario; Nancy Scott, Sault Ste. Marie; Lorne Smith, Historian, Town of Markham; Margaret and Harley Teare, Niagara-on-the-Lake; Jane Teeple, Amherstburg; Chris Tomasini and Kim Vallee, Lakehead University Library, Orillia Campus; Elizabeth Tucker, McGregor, Ontario; George Waters, Friends of

Fort York and Garrison Common; Bridget Wranich, Program Officer, Fort York National Historic Site; Marianne and Dennis Yake, descendants of militia member Daniel Yake; members of Fort Malden Volunteer Association; Orillia Public Library staff; and the Toronto Public Library staff.

W HEN THE American Revolution ended with
the signing of the Treaty of Versailles in 1783,
it ceded to the new republic of the United States "the
western country from the Allegheny Mountains to Lake
of the Woods." The treaty was considered a disaster, not
only to those who remained loyal to King George III
and Queen Charlotte but to the First Nations, the military, and the fur traders.

Why a disaster? The First Nations had been negotiating to have a large area in the "Old Northwest" (south of
Lake Erie and north of the Ohio River) declared a buffer
between Quebec (later Upper and Lower Canada) and the
new republic. The fur traders supported this plan since the
settlers and their settlements were destroying the fur trade
in the area. For those who had remained loyal to Britain,
they had lost everything — homes, farms, businesses —
and were forced to find refuge in a new homeland.

In 1783 and 1784 it is believed fifty thousand refugees streamed into the remaining British colonies to the

north. These included Newfoundland (England's oldest colony), Île Saint-Jean (Prince Edward Island), Nova Scotia, and Quebec.

This vast area had been the home of the First Nations from the beginning of time, with Britain and France struggling for control of both the territory and its rich resources. Military forts, fur-trading posts, and a chain of settlements stretched along the waterways in Nova Scotia and Quebec from the Atlantic Ocean to Lake Huron. Behind the settlements in Quebec were dense forests, and beyond lay Rupert's Land, so named since May 2, 1670, when King Charles II of England granted his cousin Prince Rupert a royal charter that gave trading rights in the area stretching from Lake Huron north to Hudson Bay, and west to the Pacific Ocean (approximately 40 percent of present-day Canada and part of the United States). The coveted "trading rights" were for furs, particularly beaver pelts.

The arrival of this enormous group of refugees who were not sojourners but settlers was to have a profound effect on a land that was already in transition. They were both Natives and newcomers, and became known as the United Empire Loyalists. Their arrival led to the partition in 1784 of the old colony of Nova Scotia into three new colonies: New Brunswick, Cape Breton Island, and a smaller Nova Scotia. Meanwhile, thousands walked north and arrived near Montreal, leading to the division of Quebec into Upper and Lower Canada in 1791.

Long before the arrival of the Loyalists, a web of human relationships had already developed among the

First Nations, explorers, fishermen, fur traders, entre-preneurs, missionaries, military, government officials, merchants, and settlers fuelled by friendship, marriage, respect, business, religion, and proximity. Now a new and strong strand was added to the landscape and to the communities developing there.

Hoping for the Best, Preparing for the Worst explores the everyday lives of those trying to survive and prosper in this sparsely populated land of astonishing harshness, beauty, and bounty in the years leading up to the War of 1812 and during the conflict. To understand the conflict it is important to travel back to the end of the American Revolution, for the seeds of the War of 1812 first sprouted there and developed over the years as implications of the Treaty of Versailles and the American lust to expand became apparent to Upper Canadians. In the interven-ing years the republic and its neighbour, Upper Canada, developed in very different ways, and we explore events in Upper Canada in the opening chapters as the stage is set for the conflict.

We begin with the arrival of the Loyalists, for they were determined to put down roots, clear forests, develop farms, open shops for trade, barter, and business, or prac-tise their professions. The men and their sons expected to plant and harvest crops, grind grain into flour, make and repair harnesses, shoes, and tin and ironware, and use all the skills they brought with them. Their mothers, wives, daughters, and sisters expected to plant, harvest, and preserve their gardens and orchards, spin and weave tex-tiles, make medicines and meals from local ingredients, and care for their families. They were not expecting war on their fields and in their forests, their homes and barns converted to hospitals, or days spent burying the dead in unmarked graves. In just over two decades those who sought refuge in Upper Canada found that they were at war again, with all the unexpected horror that it was to bring into their lives.

Many had hoped that the Treaty of Versailles, despite their disappointment with it, would bring an end to conflict, while others realized that this was simply a suspension of hostilities. During the revolution, the colonies governed from Halifax and Quebec had resisted American invasion and supported the British military efforts. The Americans, however, continued to believe the British colonies, particularly Upper Canada, were theirs for the taking — another state to add to the republic!

When war threatened, it quickly became clear that Upper Canada was the most vulnerable of the colonies, and it was believed that Upper Canada was too weak to defend itself. Its small population of less than 90,000 was scattered along the 1,300 kilometres from Cornwall on the St. Lawrence to Amherstburg on Lake Erie. The people did not grow all the food nor did they make all the goods they needed. With their own resources, they could not provide an army or even support British troops. Help from Britain in the form of men, money, supplies, and ships was essential.

All these defence needs depended on a route that the Americans could easily cut. They had only to march an army north and block the St. Lawrence south of Montreal, and Upper Canada would fall into their hands without their even having to fight there.[1]

Our focus in *Hoping for the Best, Preparing for the Worst* will be on introducing those already here and setting the stage for the inevitable war. What about the people, homes, farms, foods, and partnerships that were needed to survive in the isolation of the frontier communities that were threatened by the invasion in Upper Canada? There are four letters that help to tell the story of the land, the people, and the approach of the war. They were written by Martha to her sister, Mary, "back home" in Scotland. Martha and Mary are fictional young women, but the inn on Yonge Street where Martha worked actually existed at this period. The owner, the widowed Mrs. Vallière, her son, James Remi Vallière, her grandson, William "Bill" Cowan, and all the other people and events described in the letters are not fictional, but a part of the history of Upper Canada.[2]

Hoping for the Best, Preparing for the Worst is not about politics or the bravery of the opposing armies and their allies but about simple, everyday events and in some cases the everyday people telling their everyday stories in their own everyday words. Let us consider the land and its people as the calendars and clocks slowly moved toward June 1812.

1

....

From the Beginning of Time

FOR THOUSANDS of years before the arrival of the Europeans, the First Nations lived, travelled, and traded in the great land mass that became known as Canada. They were already heirs to millennia of experience in this vast territory and had an understanding of, and respect for, the natural world. This knowledge of the environment was crucial to their survival, and the newcomers soon appreciated its value to them in both peace and war.

The First Nations had played an important role in the American Revolution but lost their ancestral lands when Britain recognized American independence in the 1783 Treaty of Versailles and established a boundary between the new republic and what remained of British North America. The tribes thought they had been betrayed at the negotiating table, and this resulted in the local British authorities refusing to evacuate the American side of the Great Lakes frontier. The British violated the treaty by keeping their troops on American soil at the

Oswego, Niagara, Michilimackinac, and Detroit forts as well as Indian Department officials to maintain good relations with their Native allies, whom they respected as highly skilled warriors. Loyalty to the British Crown was acknowledged at the end of the revolution with grants of land for settlement.

> Whereas His Majesty having been pleased to direct that in Consideration of the early Attachment to His Cause manifested by the Mohawk Indians, & of the Loss of their Settlement they thereby sustained that a Convenient Tract of Land under His Protection should be chosen as a Safe & Comfortable Retreat for them & others of the Six Nations who have either lost their Settlements within the Territory of the American States, or wish to retire from them to the British — I have, at the earnest Desire of many of these His Majesty's faithfull Allies purchased a Tract of Land, from the Indians situated between the Lakes Ontario, Erie & Huron and I do hereby in His Majesty's name authorize and permit the said Mohawk Nation, and such other of the Six Nation Indians as wish to settle in that Quarter to take Possession of, & Settle upon the Banks of the River commonly called Ours [Ouse] or Grand River, running into Lake Erie, allotting to them for that Purpose Six Miles deep from each Side of the River beginning at Lake Erie,

& extending in that Proportion to the Head of the said River, which them & their Posterity are to enjoy for ever.

Given Under my Hand & Seal &c &c
25th Oct 1784
(Signed) Fred: Haldimand[1]

The First Nations were as diverse among their clans and nations as the newcomers, for as well as warriors, many were hunters and gatherers, fishermen, foragers, and in some areas fine farmers. They grew a mix of native and European crops that included tobacco, wheat, rye, oats, peas, potatoes, turnips, flax, and orchard fruits; and the variety of livestock they raised was similar to that found in white settlements.[2]

Their knowledge of simple cures for many medical problems was legendary. For example, they prevented and treated scurvy with cranberries, blueberries, or dandelions; plantain or fireweed leaves were used to treat wounds; maidenhair fern cured coughs and consumption, while Labrador tea eased digestive upsets.[3]

Many clans and nations had members of proven skill in the challenging art of bone-setting, and they would be called on to care for difficult and complicated fractures and dislocations. The methods often included botanic remedies, massages, or a sweat-bath.[4] They were adept at finding survival foods or creating them from natural ingredients, and this skill was to be invaluable, not only to the fur traders with whom they became partners but also to the military as the clouds of war gathered.

After John Graves Simcoe was appointed the first lieutenant governor of Upper Canada, he realized from the outset how valuable the First Nations were to him and his new government, but also how important they would be as allies in any conflict. When U.S. President James Madison declared war in 1812, the population in the Grand River community was close to two thousand, with four hundred of them warriors. Their decision to take up their weapons and join the British meant success for the British Army and Upper Canadian militia in many of the battles, and often the presence of the First Nations caused the Americans to surrender before a battle even started.

Many individuals emerged from the First Nations during the conflict as heroes and heroines, including the Shawnee chief Tecumseh; his aide-de-camp Oshahwahnoo; Joseph Brant; Brant's son, John; and many others described in detail in Carl Benn's *The Iroquois in the War of 1812*. Molly Brant, the older sister of Joseph, was the daughter of the Mohawk chief Nickus Brant and the grandniece of King Hendrick, the most powerful of all the Six Nations chiefs, and she had married Sir William Johnson in 1752 in a Mohawk ceremony.[5] Their family included Peter, Elizabeth (who married Dr. Robert Kerr), Magdalen, Margaret (who married Captain George Farley, 24th Regiment Kingston), George (who married a Cayuga girl), Mary, Susanna (who married Lieutenant Henry Lemoine), and Anne (who married Captain Hugh Earl, commodore on Lake Ontario).[6]

Molly became the highly respected "head of the Six Nations Matrons" and a Loyalist who had been harassed and lost her property during the revolution. She received land grants at Niagara, Fredericksburg, and Kingston, and both she and Joseph had homes built for them by the British military at Kingston. She was a devoted Anglican, the only woman among the donors to the first Protestant church built in Kingston in 1791.[7]

2

. . . .

"Thank God, We Are No Longer in Dread!"

Hannah, the eleven-year-old daughter of Jerusha and Sergeant Benjamin Ingraham of the King's American Regiment, recorded her family's flight from the new republic of the United States to the remaining British colonies in North America after the American Revolution and the signing of the Treaty of Versailles in 1783:

> A ship was ready to take us ... killed the cow, sold the beef, and a neighbour took home the tallow and made us a good parcel of candles and put plenty of beeswax in to make them hard and good.
>
> Uncle came down and thrashed our wheat, 20 bushels, and grandmother came and made bags for the wheat, and we packed up a tub of butter, a tub of pickles, and a good store of potatoes.[1]

The Ingrahams arrived in St. Ann's (present day Fredericton, New Brunswick) where they sheltered in tents and survived on the supplies they had brought with them augmented by government rations of flour, butter, and pork. On the morning of November 6, 1783, Hannah wrote:

When we waked we found snow lying deep on the ground all around us, and then father came wading through it and told us the house was ready and not to stop to light a fire then, and not to mind the weather, but follow his tracks through the trees, for the trees were so many that we soon lost sight of him going up the hill; it was snowing fast, and oh, so cold. Father carried a chest and we all took something and followed him up the hill through the trees to see our gable end. It was not long before we heard him pounding, and oh, what joy. There was no floor laid, no window, no chimney, no door, but we had a roof at last. A good fire was blazing in the hearth, and mother had a big loaf of bread with us, and she boiled a kettle of water and put a good piece of butter in a pewter bowl, and we toasted the bread and all said thank God, we are no longer in dread of having shots fired through our house. This is the sweetest meal I have tasted for many a day.[2]

Meanwhile, back in New York City, the last Loyalist stronghold, Michael Grass, a Mohawk Valley tanner and a former prisoner of the French during the Seven Years' War, was asked by Governor Guy Carleton (the British general commanding at New York at the end of the American Revolution): "I understand that you have been at Frontenac [present-day Kingston] in Canada. What sort of country is it? Can people live there?" Grass's response was positive: "What I saw of it I think is a fine country, and if people were settled there I think they would do very well."[3]

John Grass, the eleven-year-old son of Michael, goes on to report that when his father was asked by the governor, he agreed to take charge of a company of men, women, and children and proceed to Frontenac.

The first season they reached Sorel in Quebec where they were forced to erect huts for shelter during the winter. The next spring they took boats and reached Frontenac, pitching their tents on Indian Point to await the survey of the townships on the St. Lawrence. The Governor [Frederick Haldimand] arrived in July and the leaders chose their townships: 1st Kingston: Michael Grass; 2nd Ernestown: Sir John Johnson; 3rd Fredericksburg: Colonel [Peter] Rogers; 4th Adolphustown: Major Vanalston [Peter Van Alstine]; 5th Marysburg: Colonel Macdonnel [Archibald MacDonnell].

Before leaving, the Governor very considerately remarked to my father — "Now Mr. Grass, is it too late in the season to put in any crops? What can you do?" My father replied that if they were furnished with some turnip seed they might raise some turnips (which he pronounced durnips). Accordingly he sent some seed from Montreal, and each man taking a handful, cleared a spot of ground, about the centre of what is now the town of Kingston, sowed the seed, and raised a fine crop of turnips, which partly served for their food for the ensuing winter.[4]

Fourteen townships were soon surveyed along the St. Lawrence River, the Bay of Quinte, and the Niagara and Detroit areas for the occupation of the Loyalist refugees and the disbanded Loyalist regiments and their families.

The St. Lawrence settlers arrived too late to plant crops in 1784 and had to appeal to the government for extra supplies to see them through the first year. In 1787, just as they began to become established, they suffered crop failures and threats of famine as the Crown rations were ending. Leeks, buds of trees, and leaves were ground up to eat, and 1788 became known as the "hungry year" because of the shortage of food. One of the Loyalists reported:

While many difficulties were encountered in the early settlement, yet we realized many advantages. We were always supplied with venison; deer was plentiful, partridge and pigeons in abundance, plenty of fish for all who wished to catch them, no taxes to pay, and an abundance of wood at our doors. Although deprived of many kinds of fruit, we obtained the natural productions of the country — strawberries, raspberries, gooseberries, blackberries, and plenty of red plums. Cranberries were found in abundance in marshes. The only animal we brought with us was a dog named Tipler that proved almost invaluable in hunting.

After the first year, we raised a supply of Indian corn; but had no mill to grind it, and were, therefore, compelled to pound it in a large mortar, manufacturing what we call "Samp," which was made into Indian bread, called by the Dutch, "Suppawn." The mortar was constructed in the following manner: We cut a log from a large tree, say two and a half feet in diameter and six feet in length, planted firmly in the ground, so that about two feet projected above the surface; then carefully burned the centre of the top, so as to form a considerable cavity, which was then scraped clean. We generally selected an ironwood tree, about six inches in diameter, to form a pestle. Although this simple contrivance did well enough for corn, it did not answer for grinding wheat. The Government, seeing the difficulty, built a mill back of Kingston, where inhabitants for seven miles below Brockville got their grinding done.[5]

The Native allies from the Six Nations were settled along the Grand River under the leadership of Captain Joseph Brant, and in the Bay of Quinte area near Deseronto, under the leadership of Captain John Deseronto.

Suddenly, the area west of the Ottawa River, known for centuries as a highway for trappers and traders in search of furs, a hunting and fishing ground for thousands of Native people, and the site of a few scattered French and English forts and tiny settlements along major waterways, rang to the sound of the broadaxe and the adze as homes and farms were carved out of the wilderness.

Not everyone who survived the American Revolution and sought sanctuary in Upper Canada became permanent residents; some used it as a transfer point to settle in another part of the empire. One of those temporary residents was Elizabeth Hicks, who was born at Pedlar, near Jamestown, on the River James in Virginia on May 18, 1762. Her family farmed a large estate and refused, when the revolution began, to bear arms against the king of England.[6] When their properties were confiscated by the American government, the family fled to the Back Settlements in search of land and security. This was a 350-mile journey west, taking them beyond the Allegheny Mountains close to the Kanawha River and Falls. Despite a nearby garrison at Fort Lee and assistance from the military personnel, a series of misadventures occurred, including alarms from the First Nations and an outbreak of smallpox, taking the life of Elizabeth's mother, two younger children, Nancy and James, and a newborn infant.[7] Thirteen-year-old

Elizabeth was very ill, but eventually recovered to find that Dr. Maquire, the fort's doctor, had used his utmost skill to save her life.[8]

There were continued alarms, so the remaining household moved to the fort for security. On one of the return trips to the farm, on July 17, 1777, they were attacked by Natives and all the men were killed. Elizabeth was taken prisoner and worked as a servant in a Native [Mingo/Iroquoian] encampment and a nearby [Wyandot/descendants of Huron] community until the day Captain Henry Bird of the British Army arrived, having heard there was a young woman in distress.[9] He immediately fell in love with Elizabeth and pleaded with her to accompany him to Detroit and safety. She finally agreed despite her reluctance to travel unchaperoned with a comparative stranger! Elizabeth knew that when her family was attacked, her two sisters were to be delivered to the English at Detroit, and this might have influenced her to agree to accompany Henry Bird.

Travelling on horseback, they met and jour-neyed north with Captain Mackay and his company, accompanied by Mrs. Mackay and son Tom. Finally, they reached Detroit after a hazardous journey, and Elizabeth was established in her own quarters with a companion until her marriage to Henry was secretly arranged by Captain Mackay a few months later. In the meantime Elizabeth was befriended by many of her new acquaintances: the fort's doctor, Bet Seymour; a civilian she called Barney; and, of course, the Mackay family. Captain Bird visited Elizabeth every evening until one evening

at nine o'clock he took leave, saying that he should breakfast with me. Next morning I put on a white muslin gown, and my bonnet and veil. I had just left my room when he came in, dressed very smartly, and powdered.

"Dear me," I exclaimed, "where are you going this morning?"

"What makes you ask?"

"Because you are dressed for a field day."

"Perhaps there may be; but that was not the reason. I am to breakfast with you, and that is enough."

After breakfast was over, Barney came in and asked, "Are you ready, now?"

He said, "Yes."

Then turning to me, said, "Betsy, you will go out to-day."

As he spoke the Doctor, a stranger [who was a clergyman], Barney, and Bet came in. I was greatly surprised, then Captain Bird took my hand, and said, "My dearest girl, I wish for a short ceremony to be performed before we go out." No words can describe what I felt when the ring was put on, I sank back into a chair, and when the clergy put down the book, I darted into my dressing-room, where falling on my knees, I prayed to God to enable me to fulfil the solemn engagement which I had been drawn into so unexpectedly; and made a resolution which I have kept to the last. When they saw that I would not return they all went out. Bet came to the door, and told me they were all gone. Oh what I suffered I could never tell.

"Bet," I asked, "why did you not tell me this morning what they were going to do?"

"Because," she replied, "I did not know anything about it, if I had, you should have known it directly."

Captain Bird came to the door, Bet opened it, and he found me sitting with my elbows on the dressing-table, my head on my hands, and a handkerchief over my eyes. He put his arm round my neck, and was with one knee on the ground before I knew that he was in the room; he begged pardon for surprising me, but said, "I might have begged for months and not have gained more than I have now gained in a few hours, the surest way to victory is a surprise."[10]

Captain Bird was described by his colleagues as "one of the most active and efficient officers in the British service" who had just been promoted from the rank of lieutenant to captain when he came from Niagara to Detroit in the autumn of 1778. The garrison at Detroit was expecting an attack, and with the existing fort indefensible and in the absence of the regular engineering officer, Bird laid out the plans for

Fort Lernoult (later renamed Fort Shelby), the new fortification.

At the end of the revolution Bird and several fellow officers obtained a grant of land from the First Nations, seven miles square, at the mouth of the Detroit River. The municipal history of Amherstburg, 1784–1796, tells us Edward Hazel cleared sixteen acres on the Captain Bird lot on the future site of Fort Malden. Two log houses were built on the riverfront, one occupied by Hazel and his wife and the other by Henry Ramsay and his wife. The two women were sisters, formerly Judith and Agnes Hicks.[11]

Finally, the three sisters were reunited under the British flag their parents and their husbands loved so well.

3

"THE AMOUNT OF FLESH OR FISH REQUIRED"

W E MAY never know when the first newcomers met the First Nations and realized each group coveted something that only the other group could provide. For the newcomers it was the fine furs worn by the First Nations, while for the Natives it was the firearms, ammunition, steel knives, copper kettles, cloth, jewellery, and baubles that the Europeans traded for furs.

This meeting of cultures must have led to many surprises for the First Nations, including the arrival of independent traders in search of beaver pelts. The First Nations already hunted beaver because every part of the animal was important to them. The meat was tasty, with the tail a special treat. The fat could be skimmed off as it cooked and used to make medicines. The teeth and claws were polished for decoration and ceremonial wear, and *castoreum*, the bitter, orange-brown substance known as musk, was used to treat headaches, fevers, and aching muscles. The newcomers were interested in the pelts only. Why?

For the fur merchants in Britain and Europe, the demand for prime beaver pelts was at its height as European and Russian beavers were vanishing. The nobility was demanding fine furs for robes, jackets, capes, and muffs. Every gentleman who could afford a felt hat insisted that it must be made of the soft downy undercoat of the beaver.

Two newcomers from France, Médard Chouart Des Groseilliers and his brother-in-law Pierre Esprit Radisson, had arrived as young men and worked and travelled as explorers, coureurs de bois, and fur traders among many of the clans and nations. They were aware of the demand, realized the wealth of furs in the area surrounding Hudson Bay, and lobbied for permission to trade in that region. On May 2, 1670, King Charles II of England granted a royal charter to his cousin, Prince Rupert, including the trading rights to Rupert's Land. "The Governor and Company of Adventurers of England trading into Hudsons Bay" then controlled 40 percent of present-day Canada (from the Manitoba border to the Pacific Ocean) and some territory that is now part of the United States.

By the end of the eighteenth century, as the Ingrahams, the Glass family, and their friends, neighbours, and fellow Loyalists were becoming established on their land and building their new homes, the Hudson's Bay Company was being seriously challenged by a group of free traders who formed the North West Company. Instead of building their trading posts close to Hudson Bay and forcing the Native trappers and traders to come to them as the Hudson's Bay Company did, the North West Company came up with an ingenious plan that spanned the continent and created a partnership of newcomers (many Scottish merchants), First Nations and Métis guides (the children of Native-white marriages), and French-Canadian voyageurs.

The North West Company established an inland headquarters midway between Montreal and the far interior of the continent. The new company also built a chain of smaller forts and posts across the continent so that First Nations people would not have to travel long distances. The first inland headquarters was built at Grand Portage, but when the international boundary was redrawn after the American Revolution, the North West Company's headquarters was moved to the north shore of Lake Superior and called Fort William, with forty-two buildings set in a rectangle. To serve the everyday business of the company and the Rendezvous held every July to bring all the partners from both Montreal and the inland posts together with their servants, about two thousand in all, a farm was developed: "The land behind the fort and on both sides of it was cleared and under tillage. Barley, peas, oats, Indian corn, potatoes, as well as other grains and vegetables were grown there. Seven horses, thirty-two cows and bulls, and a large number of sheep were kept on the farm, as well."[1]

It may have been Alexander Henry, an English trader travelling on the Ottawa River in 1761, who first recorded the simple, compact rations of the voyageurs, supplied by the First Nations when they were en route to the inland headquarters:

> The village of L'Arbre Croche [twenty miles west of Fort Michilimackinac] supplies, as I have said, the maize, or Indian corn, with which the canoes are victualled. This species of grain is prepared for use, by boiling it in a strong lie, after which the husk may be easily removed; and it is next mashed and dried. In this state, it is soft and friable, like rice. The allowance, for each man, on the voyage, is a quart a day; and a bushel, with two pounds of prepared fat, is reckoned to be a month's subsistence. No other allowance is made, of any kind; not even salt; and bread is never thought of. The men, nevertheless, are healthy, and capable of performing their heavy labour. This mode of victualling is essential to the trade, which being pursued at great distances, and in vessels so small as canoes, will not admit of the use of other food. If the men were to be supplied with bread and pork, the canoe would not carry a sufficiency for six months; and the ordinary duration of the voyage is not less than fourteen. The difficulty which would belong to an attempt to reconcile any other man, than Canadians, to this fare, seems to secure to them, and their employers, the monopoly of the fur-trade.... I bought more than a hundred bushels, at forty livres per

bushel.... I paid at the rate of a dollar per pound for the tallow, or prepared fat to mix with it.[2]

To overcome the short summers and long winters in Canada, many of the partners of the company wintered in Montreal, spending their time assembling the trade goods, supervising the warehouses along the St. Lawrence River, and preparing for the year ahead. The rest of the partners manned the inland posts in the West and the far Northwest, trading and bartering directly with the First Nations for the pelts. They, too, were preparing for the year ahead. As soon as the ice was gone from the lakes and rivers, both groups started for Fort William. The inland traders used small *canots du nord*, which could be paddled by six men and portaged by two, and which held two tons of pelts and provisions for the thousand-mile journey. The Montreal merchants used Montreal canoes, or *canots du maître*, which were large freight canoes, holding four tons of freight and each requiring ten French-Canadian or Métis voyageurs as paddlers to cover approximately the same distance.[3]

The Canadian climate ensured that the chain of forts could not be reached in one short season and that rations of a different type were needed by the inland trappers and traders. The First Nations introduced them to pemmican, light, durable and highly nourishing, packed in leather bags that could easily be stored in a canoe:

> Pemmican was used on voyages in the far interior. This was a kind of pressed buffalo meat, pounded fine, to which hot grease was added, and the whole left to form a mould in a bag of buffalo skin. When properly made, pemmican would remain edible for more than one season. Its small bulk and great nutritional value made it highly esteemed by all voyageurs. From it they made a dish called "Rubbaboo"… it is a favourite dish with the northern voyageurs, when they could get it. It consists simply of pemmican made into a kind of soup by boiling water. Flour is added when it can be obtained, and it is generally considered more palatable with a little sugar.[4]

The amount of food available to the local resident traders, their families, the First Nations who bartered their pelts and often camped outside the posts, and the travellers who might find refuge has been described:

> The amount of flesh or fish required to provision even a small trading post was staggering. In one winter at Alexander Henry the Younger's Pembina [Manitoba] post, seventeen men, ten women, and fourteen children "destroyed" to use Henry's own phrase, 63,000 pounds of buffalo

meat, 1,150 fish of different kinds, some miscellaneous game, and 325 bushels of vegetables from the garden. It added up to about a ton of meat and fish for every man, woman, and child in Pembina.[5]

Travellers often noted the gardens, fields, and provisions that augmented the fishing and hunting undertaken by the men stationed at a post on a regular basis. Four travellers detailed what they observed at Fort Lac la Pluie, a North West Company post located on the Rainy River between the company's inland headquarters on Lake Superior and its remote fur posts in the Far Northwest:

There is a good garden, well stocked with vegetables of various kinds — potatoes, in particular, which are now eatable.[6]

We saw here cultivated fields and domestic animals, such as horses, oxen, cows, &c.[7]

Oats and wheat were grown and later processed at the water-powered gristmill at Chaudière Falls.[8]

A very important food staple for many of the forts was wild rice, often called wild oats by the fur traders:

This useful grain is produced in no other part of the North West Country.... It grows in water about two feet deep, where there is a rich muddy bottom ... in appearance bears a considerable resemblance to oats.... This grain is gathered in such quantities, in this region, that in ordinary seasons, the North West Company purchase annually, from twelve to fifteen hundred bushels of it, from the Natives; and it constitutes a principal article of food, at the posts in the vicinity.[9]

Despite their ongoing competition, the men in the vast tracts of wilderness they served for their companies often reached out in friendship on some occasions, for we learn from John McKay, newly arrived at the neighbouring Hudson's Bay Company post, of an extraordinary gift he received from competitor Charles Boyer, the North West Company clerk at Fort Lac la Pluie:

I opened the parsal Mr. Boyer made me a present of which was coverd with a well Dressed moose skin. it contained a case of Mathematical Instruments a small Slate 2 pewter Barom 2 phials of Pepermint 2 do. [ditto] of Turlingtons Balsam of Life 1 do. Essce [essence] Bingamat 1 do. Essce lemon 1 do. hungary water a Steel watch Chain with a Silver Seal and 2 pound of Chocolate.[10]

A fine welcome to a competitor as the celebration of Christmas approached on that December day in 1793!

The key partners of the North West Company were Scotsmen, many of them Highland gentlemen with an army of six hundred voyageurs — hardy, serviceable, intrepid, inured to danger, amenable to discipline, and obedient to instructions. When war with the United States was declared, they immediately formed one of the most useful, active, and efficient regiments, the Corps de Voyageurs Canadien, with Scottish Highland officers and French-Canadian voyageur servicemen. They were to have a profound effect on coming events.[11]

4

"THE APPREHENSION OF WAR"

COLONEL JOHN Graves Simcoe had served with the Queen's Rangers in the American Revolution and wanted to bring to his new posting of lieutenant governor of Upper Canada the British principles and benefits the Americans had rejected. He was accompanied by his wife, Elizabeth Posthuma Gwillim, and their two youngest children, Sophia, two years, and Francis, three months old. Their four oldest daughters, Eliza, Charlotte, Henrietta, and Caroline, were left at home with their friend, Mrs. Ann Hunt, and her daughter, Mary, as governess and tutor.[1]

In preparation for their arrival and the hope of a comfortable home, two "canvas houses" with wooden frames and floorboards were purchased at the auction of the late Captain James Cook's effects, along with several conventional tents.[2] They sailed on His Majesty's frigate *Triton* on September 26, 1791, and anchored at Quebec City on November 11 after a turbulent voyage of six weeks.

Elizabeth was a keen observer, interested in botany and trained as an artist with pencil, pen, and watercolours. Like so many other gentlewomen of the period, she kept a diary and created vivid word pictures as well as her sketches of the hardships of the voyage, their arrival and search for lodgings, everyday life, illnesses, accidents, medicines, foods, and beverages, for nothing escaped her notice and her notebook!

They wintered in Quebec and enjoyed the social round — suppers, dinners, teas, balls, concerts, assemblies, walks, drives, and church services. On Monday, December 26, "the Division of the Province into Upper Canada & Lower Canada & the new Constitution given to the former was announced by Proclamation," Elizabeth reported. "There were dinners at the Hotels & illuminations at night to commemorate the event." The following day she wrote: "I was at a very pleasant Ball at the Chateau & danced with Prince Edward [who became the Prince of Wales and the father of Queen Victoria]."[3]

A few days later on New Year's Eve the first indication of events to come were recorded by Elizabeth:

Accounts received from Montreal of the defeat of 2000 of the people of the U. States about 20 miles from the Miami Fort, by 1400 Indians. They had barricaded their Camp with flour barrels etc. The Indians attacked them, beat them, & took 6 pieces of Cannon, all their provisions, new clothing, etc., killed 1200 men. The Indians lost only 50 men.[4]

Simcoe was constantly concerned that an invasion was coming from the new republic, and Elizabeth expressed her concern on many occasions: "The apprehension of War with the U. States engages my attention very disagreeably."[5]

She realized that there was a complex web of relationships already in place for, as they left Quebec for the temporary capital at Newark, she admired "the Song of the Batteaux men.... This practice has been learned from Grand Voyageurs, or Canadians who are hired by the N. West Company to take Canoes to the Grand Portage beyond Lake Superior."[6]

On many occasions she also remarked that her husband, "the Governor," or "His Excellency," or "Coll. Simcoe," praised the First Nations for their skill and knowledge in his service as he travelled the new province (much of it on foot), searching for an appropriate site for the capital. At one point he was convinced that a spot on La Tranche River (present-day London on the Thames River) was ideal:

The Gov. rose early on the march & walked till 5 o'clock. A party of the Indians went on an hour before to cut down wood for a fire & make Hutts of trees which they cover with bark so dexterously that no rain can penetrate, & this they do very expeditiously; when the Gov. came to the spot the Indians had fixed upon to Lodge for the night the Provision was cooked, after Supper the Officers sung God Save the

King & went to sleep with their feet close to an immense fire which was kept up all night. The Gov. found his expectations perfectly realized as to the goodness of the Country on the banks of the La Tranche, & is confirmed in his opinion that the forks of the Thames is the most proper scite for the Capital of the Country, to be called New London on a fine dry plain without underwood but abounding in good Oak Trees.[7]

The rumours of war continued, however, and Elizabeth resolved to visit her friends in Quebec in the fall of 1794 and was not sure if she would return to Upper Canada "if the question of peace or war was not speedily settled."[8]

After entertaining the ladies of the garrison at Niagara to tea, she began her preparations for Quebec and embarked on the schooner *Mississauga* with her family on September 13, 1794. She had a very agreeable travelling companion in Molly Brant, the older sister of Joseph Brant, and the widow of Sir William Johnson. Molly took up residence in Kingston while Elizabeth and her family proceeded to Lower Canada. On an April afternoon in 1796, the bell in the tower of St. George's Anglican church tolled its solemn message of farewell to Molly, the woman who in the difficult years following the revolution persuaded the First Nations to remain loyal to their king.[9]

Despite her concern about war, Elizabeth did return to Upper Canada and moved between York and Niagara where on June 12, 1796, Elizabeth told of her visit to the home of Adam Green and his family:

> They prepared me some refreshment at this house; some excellent cakes, baked on the coals; eggs; a boiled black squirrel; tea, and coffee made of peas, which was good; they said coffee was better. The sugar was made from black walnut trees, which looks darker than that from the maple but I think is sweeter.
>
> Green's wife died a year ago and left ten children, who live here with their father in a house consisting of a room, a closet and a loft; but being New Jersey people, their house is delicately clean and neat, and not the appearance of being inhabited by three people, every part is so neatly kept.[10]

We will learn more about Green's children when war is declared and the American army arrives in Stoney Creek.

In September 1796, Elizabeth, her husband, and their family returned to England aboard the *Pearl*. We owe a debt of gratitude to Elizabeth, who recorded so many details of everyday life, including her meals, whether taken out of doors, in the large bower composed of oak boughs, the canvas house, tents, huts, under umbrellas, in the marquee, or as a guest at someone else's table, as the diary contains scores of references to "taking tea," "supping," "dining," and "breakfasting." Fortunately, she often tells us what was on the table, including wild geese, turkeys, partridges, pigeons, ducks, snipes, woodcock, elk, caribou, bear, racoon, porcupine, pickerel, cod, eel, black bass, pike, whitefish, sturgeon, perch, herrings, salmon, swordfish, tortoise, rattlesnake, wild rice, and much more!

Wild fruits and nuts were in abundance, including gooseberries, apples (fresh and dried), strawberries, raspberries, plums, grapes, whortleberries, watermelon, hurtleberries, cranberries, cherries, peaches, butternuts, and chestnuts.[11]

Both Newark and York, to which the capital was moved in 1796, because of the fear of invasion, might have been small settlements, but the residents enjoyed a busy social round of activities, and it would be there that "made" dishes would be served, such as cakes, sweet-meats, cold tongue, chowder, pumpkin pie, mock turtle soup, and some very good cakes.[12]

5

"In the Shelter of the Fort"[1]

A S THE nineteenth century began, a classic pattern of settlement was still apparent in Upper Canada, for settlers had often sought the protection of the garrison in choosing land and planting crops and erecting homes, mills, schools, and churches. The forts or posts (whether military or fur trade) were often the mainstay of the economy, and despite their many changes in ownership and name (both fort and community), they were the focus of social life and entertainment.

In the beginning, Kingston was called Cataraqui or Cataracoui or Katarakoui or Cataracouy by the First Nations, later Catarakwe by the French. For more than three hundred years it had been the home of a garrison, first French, then English, guarding the entrance to the St. Lawrence River and the Great Lakes, as well as the chain of small lakes and rivers leading to the Ottawa River and the richest fur country in the world.

The garrison was named Fort Frontenac in honour of "the Fighting Governor," Compte de Louis de Buade

Frontenac, and the community that grew up around it was named Kingston in honour of King George III. It was here that

> Captain Michael Grass, who had once been a prisoner in Fort Frontenac, led in some of the first parties of Loyalist exiles. The King's Royal Regiment of New York — mostly Highlanders from the Mohawk Valley lands of the Johnsons — was disbanded at the head of the river and other families straggled in, some of them half-naked and starving. The head of each family was given a tent and a ticket giving him a draw in the land lottery: one hundred acres of forested wilderness in his own name and fifty for each member of his family (the officers naturally drew first). Every two families got a cross-cut saw and sets of other tools and supplies of seed wheat were thinly spread.[2]

By 1792, when the Simcoes arrived en route to the temporary capital at Newark, Elizabeth recorded:

Sunday, July 1st

> Kingston is six leagues from Gananowui, a small town of about fifty wooden Houses and Merchants' Store Houses. Only one house is built of stone, it belongs to a Merchant. There is a

small Garrison here, & a harbour for ships. They fired a salute on our arrival, & we went to the House appointed for the Commanding Officer, at some distance from the Barracks.... The Queen's Rangers are encamped ¼ mile beyond our House, and the bell Tents have a very pretty appearance. The situation of this place is entirely flat, & incapable of being rendered defensible, therefore, were its situation more central, it would still be unfit for the seat of Government.[3]

A short time later François Liancourt described the town:

It consists of about one hundred and twenty or one and thirty houses. The ground in the immediate vicinity of the city rises with a gentle swell and forms, from the lake onward, as it were, an amphitheatre of lands cleared, but not yet cultivated. None of the buildings are distinguished by a more handsome appearance from the rest. The only structure, more conspicuous than the others, and in front of which an English flag is hoisted, is the barracks, a stone building, surrounded with pallisadoes.

All the houses stand on the northern bank of the bay, which stretches a mile farther into the country. On the southern bank are the buildings belonging to the naval force, the wharfs, and the habitations of all the persons who belong to that department. The King's ships lie at anchor near these buildings, and consequently have a harbour and road separate from the port for merchantmen.

Kingston, considered as a town, is much inferior to Newark; the number of houses is nearly equal in both. Kingston may contain a few more buildings, but they are neither so large nor so good as at Newark. Many of them are log houses and those which consist of joiners work are badly constructed and painted. But few new houses are built. No Town Hall, no Court House, and no prison have hitherto been constructed. The houses of two or three merchants are conveniently situated for loading and unloading ships; but, in point or structure, these are not better than the rest. Their trade chiefly consists in peltry, which comes across the lake and in provision from Europe, with which they supply Upper Canada. They act as agents or commissioners of the Montreal Company, who have need of magazines in all places, where their goods must be unshipped.

The trade of Kingston, therefore, is not very considerable. The merchant ships are only three in number, and make but eleven voyages in a year. Kingston is the staple port. It is situated twelve miles above that point of the river, which is considered the extremity of the lake. Here arrive all the vessels, which sail up the river of

St. Lawrence, laden with provision brought in European ships to Quebec.[4]

It was René-Robert Cavelier de la Salle who had been instructed by Frontenac to build the forts at Cataraqui and Niagara that were to be, the French believed, the first in a chain of stepping stones to their new kingdom of the central rivers. In 1758 the French lost Cataraqui, and the following year lost their three-storey stone fort at Niagara. The main building resembled a French château:

> Built of stone blocks, four feet thick, three stories high, 105 feet long, its narrow barred windows were planned for defence and cannon were placed to be fired from the dormers above. It had an inside well and its total cost was nearly $6000, in current value — a great sum in the eighteenth century.... The fort proper covered about eight acres and had its ravines, ditches, and pickets curtains, counterscarps and covered way; stone towers, laboratory and magazine; web-house, barracks, baker, and blacksmith shop. For worship there was a chapel with a large dial over the door to mark the course of the sun. The dungeon, called the "black hole," was a strong, dark and dismal place; and in one corner of the room was affixed the apparatus for strangling such unhappy wretches as fell under the displeasure of the despotic rulers of those days.[5]

An army marches on its stomach, so the provisions for these forts were crucial:

> From 1760 to 1796, the British at Niagara would plant gardens and orchards with seed provided from Europe. Crops included beets, peas, carrots, beans, onions, cabbage, turnips and lettuce. The British were slow to accept potatoes as a foodstuff. It is interesting to note that they were not grown at Niagara until the time of the American Revolution (1775–83), but, by 1778, potatoes were being eaten by the fort's population. From 1782 to 1796, the garrison provided the chief financial support for the local farmers. Indeed, men such as Robert Hamilton, Richard Cartwright and Robert Nichol provided the commissariat department with flour, vegetables and Indian corn in amounts large enough to make them wealthy.[6]

Fort Niagara had commanded the mouth of the Niagara River for close to a century. During the revolution, it had been the bulwark of the British defence of the Great Lakes. The isolation of Fort Niagara had since its construction made movement and supply of provisions both difficult and expensive:

> The needs of the troops had to be projected as much as two years in advance. This had to be

done accurately and without delay, in order to give government agents time to purchase, package and ship the foodstuffs to America. Then, loaded aboard sailing vessels, the provisions of Niagara's French and British soldiers were transported thousands of miles to Quebec, subject to numerous delays and problems. The most significant of these delays was the cold North American winter which effectively isolated Fort Niagara each year from December until late April.

Once safely at Quebec, the barrels were inspected for damage. At this point they were often left open, exposed to corruption and theft by the quartermasters and laborers. Sometimes the load had been packaged in a container too large to be transported to the post. In this case, the food had to be repacked, at great cost and risk of pilferage, in order to continue its journey.

At this point, the "victuals" were loaded aboard small river craft such as bateaux and canoes, to begin the second phase of the voyage to Niagara. The containers were generally barrels, made of wood, and bound with wooden or metal straps. Barrels were produced in different sizes to contain diverse produce. Salt pork, the most typical meat sent to Fort Niagara (and eaten by all three armies — French, British and American), was shipped in 215-pound barrels. Peas and rice were transported in "tierces," each holding up to 531 pounds, and butter in "firkins" of 66 and three-quarters of a pound.[7]

The village between Fort Niagara and the river was known during the British period as "The Bottom" and provided homes to the sutlers and merchants at Niagara. These people sold to the soldiers at the garrison and traded with the local Indians. A number of storehouses, stables, a brewery (for spruce beer), root cellars, and public houses in "The Bottom" provided Fort Niagara's residents with a ready supply of food, drink and goods not normally issued by the military.[8]

Fort Niagara was never attacked during the American Revolution, but its supply of foodstuff was severely strained when First Nations and Loyalist refugees descended on the stronghold. One of the outbuildings, the Bakehouse, had two French beehive ovens and, along with other nearby ovens, could produce bread for as many as five thousand people each day. In addition, Lieutenant-General Haldimand instructed the commandant at Niagara to provide seeds and tools to a small number of Loyalist soldiers so they could clear farms across the river from the fort, which they did with very successful results.

When Fort Niagara was very close to the deadline of transfer to American control, the decision was made to construct blockhouses and storehouses on the west bank of the Niagara River where it flows into Lake Ontario. This was to become known as Fort George:

> The initial phase included the large "central" blockhouse which served as both storehouse and quarters, a stone powder magazine (which still stands), and a number of smaller structures. Sometime during 1796 the new post was named Fort George in honour of the king. Construction of additional blockhouses, officers' quarters, and other buildings would continue for the rest of the decade. The scattered buildings were enclosed by a stockade and earthen bastions in 1799, giving Fort George its familiar extended hexagon form.[9]

The surrounding settlement was originally a temporary farming community designed to provide food to Fort Niagara, but as it grew and prospered the Loyalist farmers eventually received ownership of the land after a great deal of controversy. The arrival of surveyors and the lieutenant governor with his entourage caused the town's first building boom, and in 1794, John Graves Simcoe "bragged to his superiors that the town had contained only one or two dwellings on his arrival now 'by the temporary residence of the Government' contained 'upwards of fifty houses.'"[10] Most of the new building was initiated by government and military officials stationed in the recently renamed town of Newark (formerly Niagara).

Fort Erie was originally built so close to the Niagara River that it was destroyed by huge, grinding chunks of ice, while the second building was carried away in a fierce Lake Erie storm in 1803. The third fort was built of stone on higher ground to accommodate three hundred men. Originally a simple square with four corner bastions, it was later altered by the Americans into the shape of a star. Lodgings for the officers, soldiers, commissaries, and kitchen staff were within the fort, while gardens for the officers, soldiers, artillery, and sergeants were outside the walls. The victuallers' lodging and garden, the stables and sheep pen, were in close proximity to the fort.[11]

Located strategically between Fort Niagara on the north and Fort Erie on the south, Chippawa, a strong, established military post on the Niagara River since 1791, was flanked by a "mean village of twenty houses, three stores, two taverns, a windmill and a distillery that had grown up around the garrison."[12]

The river, its military posts, and the location of Niagara Falls had made this one of the most important water and portage routes in Upper Canada. Elizabeth Simcoe noted the route as soon as she arrived in Niagara in July 1792:

M. 30th

At 8 this morning we set off in Calashes to go to the Falls 16 miles from hence. We stopped & breakfasted at Mr. Hamilton's, a merchant who lives 6 miles from here at the landing (Queenstown), where the Cargoes going to Detroit are landed & sent by land 9 miles to Ft. Chippewa.[13]

What of the other forts in the "upper country" — Michilimackinac and Detroit? The area around Michilimackinac was well-known, for in 1761 Alexander Henry wrote about the village of L'Arbre Croche, twenty miles west of Michilimackinac, and described the enormous quantity of maize or Indian corn that the First Nations produced to sell to the fur traders. In 1793, William Jarvis wrote in a letter to his father-in-law, Samuel Peters: "My cock-loft contains some of the finest maple sugar I ever beheld, 10,000 lbs was made in an Indian village near Michilimackinac. I have 150 lbs of it."

Michilimackinac was an outpost described by James Long in the eighteenth century. James left England in April 1768 aboard the *Canada* to begin a new life as an Indian interpreter and trader for a merchant based in Montreal. For the next fifteen years he lived, travelled, traded, and described his life among the First Nations and the communities in British North America. As a newcomer, his description of Michilimackinac confirmed the importance of the location for the posts that were built, moved, lost, and retaken over the years in the upper Great Lakes region:

The last post is Michillimakinac, which is situated between Lake Huron and Lake Michigan, upon an isthmus, about one hundred and thirty leagues long, and twenty-two wide, and is the last fortress towards the north-west....

This is perhaps the most material of all the barriers, and of the greatest importance to the commercial interests of this country, as it intercepts all the trade of the Indians of the upper country from Hudson's Bay to Lake Superior ...[14]

Due to the struggles to control the area and the resulting treaties, the fort was moved several times, and as the nineteenth century began, it was ceded to the Americans, prompting the British to build a new post, Fort St. Joseph, on St. Joseph's Island. The North West Company followed and established a canoe-building post, with craftsmen such as blacksmiths and others needed for the trade.

For centuries the Detroit River area called Wawyachtenok was home to the Huron Nation, and when French missionaries and settlers arrived, it was known as DeTroett, "the most beautiful and plentiful inland place in America." In 1701 a brigade of fifty soldiers and fifty voyageurs and a number of First Nations arrived by canoe led by Antoine de Lamothe Cadillac to establish a major French outpost on the Detroit River to replace Michilimackinac as the capital of the upper country. Originally called Fort Pontchartrain du Détroit, it was surrounded by a palisade to protect the Church of Saint Anne as well as the log houses constructed close by.

Under the protection of Fort Pontchartrain, settlements were gradually made on both sides of the river. In 1728 a Jesuit priest arrived at Detroit, and soon after established a Huron mission on the opposite shore, where the village of Sandwich grew up many years later. The mission-house, part of which remained until the early years of the present century, was built partly of hewed pine and partly of sawn lumber, and measured thirty by forty-five feet. In later years a church was erected, and also a priest's residence, a store-house for furs and one for provisions, and a blacksmith shop.

The settlement of the Canadian shore of the river was most extensive during the last thirty years of the French period. Numerous land grants were made between 1734 and 1756 to prospective settlers, many of them ex-soldiers, and these men erected their small homes in straggling shore settlements, as in Quebec.[15]

With the Treaty of Versailles, Fort Detroit was ceded to the new republic and finally turned over to them in 1796. By then Fort Detroit was surrounded by a palisade of twenty-three-inch cedar planks and a twelve-foot-wide moat. A town constructed almost entirely of wood had grown up around it to serve a population of about forty-five hundred, while the fort housed twenty-five hundred soldiers, the same number of muskets, and thirty-three cannon. Because of the placement of the original French homes along the river, the town had grown up between the fort and the river. This meant that the fort's guns had to fire over the rooftops of the town to reach any enemy ships on the river.

With the surrender of Fort Detroit to the Americans in 1796, a new fort, originally called Fort Amherstburg, later changed to Fort Malden, was hastily built eighteen miles south at the mouth of the river, and the guns and military stores were moved there. A visitor described the garrison town of Amherstburg where he "found about twenty houses near the fort." He states that there were also a few dwellings at the lower end of the district, and that the Detroit River was "crowded with Indian canoes, bateaux and sailing-ships, and several pleasure boats of the officers of the garrison of the new Fort Malden."[16]

At least one of the buildings in Amherstburg has a very romantic oral history surrounding it. It was said to have been built at the mouth of the Rouge River in Detroit by a family of Loyalists, and when the fort was ceded in 1796, the owners crossed the river to the new British post at Malden. When they received a land grant in 1798, they dismantled their home and towed it down-river by canoe to be reassembled on Lot 17, First Street, in the new town of Amherstburg. Mystery shrouds the ownership of Lot 17, because a draw was held in 1798 for lots on First Street and it went to the mercantile firm of Leith, Shepherd, and Duff. By August 17 of that year, the house stood on Lot 17! In 1804 the property was owned by the Mackintosh family, and a military plan of Amherstburg shows the house and gives an evaluation not only of the house but of a storehouse and wharf, as well. In *View of Amherstburg in 1813*, painted by Margaret Reynolds, we can assure ourselves that it was not a myth or simply local romantic folklore, for it is clearly visible.[17]

As other Loyalist settlers were also forced to abandon Detroit, many moved to the newly purchased Huron Reserve after drawing lots for one acre of Crown land. One thousand acres were purchased from the First Nations by the Honourable Peter Russell on behalf of the Executive Council of Upper Canada for this purpose.

Streets were laid out to replace the former farmland, and the emerging hamlet was called Sandwich after Russell's ancestral home in England. Scottish fur trader Alexander Duff left Detroit to build a new three-storey Georgian house that he also used for trade on Mill Street facing the river in 1798. Nine years later he sold his property to the Honourable James (Jacques) Bâby and retired to the shores of Lake Erie. During the hostilities, in Bâby's absence, the American Generals Hull, and later Harrison, occupied it and scavenged everything movable.[18]

For centuries the north shore of Lake Ontario between the two rivers that became known as the Humber on the west and the Don on the east, with the best natural harbour on Lake Ontario, was home to the First Nations. At first they were hunters, gatherers, and fishermen, but eventually Native farmers settled and communities grew to take advantage of the lake and the waterways for travel and trade. The fur trade prompted the building of posts and forts by the newcomers, including Fort Rouillé (called locally Fort Toronto). By the middle of the eighteenth century, the soldiers had cleared three hundred acres of land around the fort, decreasing the chances of an ambush but providing rich land for a large garden to supply food for the fort.[19]

When John Graves Simcoe arrived in Upper Canada and began to search for a safer location for the capital, its accompanying garrison, and its naval arsenal, old Fort Rouillé was in ruins and much of the post's former importance as a trade centre, harbour, and portage route was forgotten. Governor Guy Carleton (Lord Dorchester) remembered the old fort's former value and arranged to legally purchase 250,880 acres of land from the Mississauga Nation for £1,700, several barrels of cloth, some axes, and odds and ends "dear to the heart of the simple savage."[20] This was called the Toronto Purchase, which the British considered final, while the First Nations did not and continued to camp, hunt, and carry out everyday activities in the area.

After exploring other sites, on May 13, 1793, Elizabeth recorded that "Coll Simcoe returned from Toronto & speaks in praise of the harbour & a fine spot near it covered with large Oak which he intends to fix upon as a scite for a Town."[21] Simcoe dispatched the Queen's Rangers to clear brush and build huts for the military close to the location of old Fort Rouillé. By August, Augustus Jones was surveying a series of lots on the shore of the lake from St. John's Creek (now called the Humber River) eastward, leaving room for proposed roadways, and Simcoe was renaming the future capital York. There are conflicting memories of the reason for the change of name:

Did you know that the City of Toronto might have been called Dublin had it not been for the stubborn objections of one of its earliest and most prominent citizens? I certainly didn't, until I read the other day a history of the Denison family. It seems that John Denison, the first of the family to come out here from York, England, became fed up with the pioneer life and was about to return home. For one thing, he was dissatisfied with his grant of 200 acres of land, "deeming it too small to sit down upon." He wanted at least 1,000 acres.

The history describes John Denison's visit to Navy Hall at Niagara in April of 1793: "It [Navy Hall] had no charms from an architectural standpoint, and was as crude and primitive as the log cabins of the pioneers," says the account of Mr. Denison's arrival from Kingston. "Entering Navy Hall, Denison craved an audience with his old friend Peter Russell. As it happened Governor Simcoe himself was there, too. Denison told of his dissatisfaction with pioneer life and his intention to return home to York, England. He felt it behooved him to make this known, since he had come on the solicitation of Russell and Russell's sister, and could not return without notifying them. The Governor expressed deep regret at his decision, thinking privily that colonists of Denison's type were difficult enough to induce to come to

Canada in the first place and were a real loss to the country if they did not remain.

"'You may not like Kingston,' said Simcoe, 'but you have not seen the new capital of Upper Canada which we are building — the town of Dublin.'

"'Dublin!' quoth Denison. 'You have your audacity to ask a Yorkshireman like myself to set foot in a place called Dublin, of all names.'

"'Very well,' replied Simcoe. 'You name it for us, Denison. We will call it any name you suggest, provided we have your promise to remain in Canada.'

"'In that case,' said Denison, 'call it York. I said I was going to York. Call it York and I will go there and settle.'

"Simcoe and Denison were both true to their word. Denison went to York and settled and Simcoe named the new place York to satisfy Denison. On May 2, 1793, the name was officially published as York. Of course it was gazetted to be in honor of the Duke of York, who had won notable victories in Flanders, but in actual fact it owed its name to this incident ..."[22]

Later that summer a new survey for the town was prepared by Alexander Aitken, comprising a ten-block grid bounded by the present George, Berkeley, Adelaide, and Front Streets, with King Street to be the main thoroughfare. North of Lot (Queen) Street a range of hundred-acre lots stretched north to Bloor Street, to be granted to officials as gifts, in particular as compensation for moving to the new capital.[23] Lot Street was also the baseline from which the concessions of York Township stretched north, east, and west. When it became known that York would be the capital, craftsmen, industries, merchants, and those with special skills joined the reluctant members of government and their families arriving from Niagara.

In retrospect it is amazing to learn how friendly the garrisons of the Americans and British remained until the very day of, and sometimes beyond, the declaration of war in June 1812. "The American commanding officer advised the commandant at Fort St. Joseph that his men would be welcome to send correspondence to Upper Canada by way of the 'express' between Michilimackinac and Detroit. As late as 1807, the British loaned 20 barrels of pork to the Americans when they were in short supply."[24] In at least one case the friendship continued between the garrisons as war clouds deepened, for

In the officers' mess at Fort George, where the Niagara River pours into Lake Ontario, the gentlemen of the 41st Regiment were lunching with their American counterparts from Fort Niagara, a bugle call across the water. Major General Isaac Brock, Commanding Officer of Upper Canada, had just arrived after an overnight boat trip from York to announce the declaration of war by the United States against Great Britain. Of course, he added, he would insist that the regiments' guests finish their meal. Later, the officers strolled down to the riverbank, shook hands with their guests and bade them good-bye as they were rowed away. It was June 26, 1812.[25]

War had been declared eight days earlier!

"When the Journey's over There'll Be Time Enough to Sleep"[1]

FOR THOUSANDS of years the most important ways to travel in the land that became known as Canada were by foot or by watercraft. The territory was traversed by trails, paths, and great east-west rivers and included chains of lakes that became the highways of the First Nations in their canoes — dugouts, elm bark or birch bark, were the most common. The latter became the vehicles that carried the fur traders to success, as well as the newcomers who began to arrive as lines of transport lengthened. The North West Company required both large freight canoes, *canots de maîtres*, that could move up to four tons of trade goods and supplies between their headquarters in Montreal and inland headquarters at Grand Portage and Fort William, and smaller *canots du nord* to bring the inland traders and their furs from posts in the Far Northwest to the Rendezvous at the inland headquarters every summer. Whether large or small, the vessels were comparatively light in weight, but very strong with a spruce frame covered with bark and sealed with spruce resin.

Transportation on the St. Lawrence River with its numerous dangerous and unpredictable rapids demanded a different solution, and the flat-bottomed bateau (*bateaux, batteaux, batto[e]*) came into use with the crew propelling it with poles, oars, or sails, sometimes wading beside it or dragging it with ropes from the shore. Sailing vessels were also built and in use on the Great Lakes by the end of the eighteenth century. Elizabeth Simcoe reported visiting the shipyard at Kingston and the vessels there:

> The present establishment of Vessels on this Lake consists of the Onondaga & Mississaga top-sailed schooners of [about 80] tons & the Caldwell which is a Sloop. They transport all the Troops & Provisions from hence for the Garrison of Niagara, Fort Erie & Detroit. They land them at Niagara from whence those for the higher Ports are forwarded 9 miles across a Portage by Land to Fort Chippeway, 3 miles above the Falls of Niagara from whence they are embarked in boats & carried 18 miles to Ft. Erie, from whence Vessels take them to Detroit at the extremity of Lake Erie which is 300 miles in length.[2]

On land the First Nations established well-marked and well-used paths and trails beside many waterways and through the forests to reach other communities and hunting and fishing grounds. They had also introduced the newcomers to snowshoes and toboggans as well as to sleds pulled by dog teams. Simcoe initiated the brushing and constructing of several rough roads to augment the few short ones in existence, including Montreal to Kingston, Kingston to York, from York southwest to the forts of the Thames River, and another to link York to Lake Simcoe. The North West Company contributed to the construction of the last cited and began hauling their great canoes from Lake Ontario to Lake Simcoe over this route. Simcoe also authorized the construction of Dundas Street to link Lake Ontario with the Detroit area.

This was a country whose people were on the move, despite the obstacles that included the poor trails and roads and often the lack of accommodation. Mrs. Simcoe shared a description of one of her many meals while visiting Niagara Falls on August 24, 1795: "I rested myself at Painter's House where they prepared besides Tea those Cakes baked in a few minutes on an Iron before the fire which the people of the States make so well, eggs & sweetmeats & bacon or salt fish they usually offer with Tea. I believe it is a more substantial Meal with them than their dinner which is slight."[3]

Just two days later she wrote about a very different adventure and a very natural mistake:

> 25th The Gov. & I & Francis went in the Carriage to Fort Chippeway but finding the Baggage had not arrived could proceed no further, dined & slept at Capt. Hamilton's who commands

here. We walked this evening & I made some sketches, the Weather excessively hot, the Gov. very ill. We slept in a Room in the Block House where the Logs were some distance apart. Without this contrivance used as loop Holes in case of attack, as well as for admitting air, I think the heat would have been insufferable; as it was I left my bed & lay on the floor.

26th Went out early in the Boat with Capts. Darling & Smith. The latter brought me a Thermometer I had been long wishing for & the Gov. bought it of an Officer going to England, almost immediately it fell out of my hand and was broken to my great vexation. The Gov. set out on Horseback but finding himself very ill made signs from the Shore to the Boat to come ashore which we did half way between the Chippeway & Ft. Erie & at a very good farm House he stay'd the whole of the day till 6 in the Evening when we proceeded in the barge to Ft. Erie. We ordered dinner & made ourselves quite at home here supposing it an Inn, & afterwards found we were mistaken. It was not an Inn but the House of a very hospitable Farmer.[4]

In June the following year the Simcoes travelled to the Head of Lake Ontario and stayed at the King's Head Inn, which Elizabeth described:

This house was built by the Governor to facilitate communication between Niagara and the La Tranche, where he intended to establish the seat of government, and its situation was not without reference to a military position.[5]

There are eight rooms in this house, besides two low wings behind it, joined by a colonnade, where are the offices. It is a pretty plan. I breakfasted in a room to the S.E., which commands the view of the lake on the south shore, of which we discern the Point of the Forty-Mile Creek, Jones' Point and some other houses. From the rooms to the N.W. we see Flamborough Head and Burlington Bay. The sand cliffs on the north shore of Burlington Bay look like red rocks. The beach is like a park covered with large, spreading oaks. At eight o'clock we set out in a boat to go to Beasley's, at the head of Burlington Bay, about eight miles. [Richard Beasley was an Indian trader and the first settler on the land that became known as "Head of the Lake."] The river and bay were full of canoes; the Indians were fishing, we bought some fine salmon of them.[6]

Among the first business men in the growing villages and towns and along the roads and waterways were the innkeepers. Probably the first at York was Abner Miles, who kept a daybook and recorded events, charges, and debts:

Messrs. Bâby and Hamilton and Commodore Grant are jointly billed in July, 1798, for "twenty-two dinners at Eight shillings, £8 16s. Sixteen to Coffee, £1 12s. Eight Suppers, 16s. Twenty-three quarts and one pint of wine, £10 11s. 6d. Eight bottles of porter, £2 8s. Two bottles of syrup-punch, £1 4s. One bottle of brandy and one bottle of rum, 18s. Altogether amounting to £26 5s. 6d." (The amounts are in New York Currency, in which the shilling was seven pence half-penny.)

Among other events in Miles' Hotel was a "St. John's Dinner," for which Thomas Ridout, Jonathan Scott, Colonel Fortune, Surveyor Jones, Samuel Heron, Mr. Secretary Jarvis, Adjutant McGill and Mr. Crawford are each charged 16s. Chief Justice Elmsley was a prominent patron of the establishment, as was also Judge Powell. A reverend traveller's call at the inn is entered: "Priest from River La Tranche, 3 quarts corn and half-pint wine. Breakfast, 2s. 6d.," a notably frugal order in comparison with the others.[7]

William Cooper's "Toronto Coffee House" was advertised December 12, 1801 as ready for business. This combined inn and general store was probably located on Wellington St. Customers were promised "genteel board and lodging," and "the best liquors, viands, etc." In November, 1802, Cooper inserted the following advertisement in the *York Gazette*:

"Toronto Coffee House — William Cooper begs leave to acquaint his friends and the public that he has erected a large and convenient stable on his own lot opposite the Toronto Coffee House, and stored it well with hay and oats of the very best quality. Travellers will meet with genteel and comfortable accommodation at the above house, and their horses will be carefully attended to.

"He has just received from New York a large supply of the best wines, brandy, Hollands shrub, fresh lime juice, London porter, oysters, anchovies, red herrings, Devonshire, Navy and Cavis sauces, segars, pipes and tobacco. He has also received a very general assortment of groceries and dry goods, which he will sell cheap for cash or exchange for country produce."[8]

Innkeepers played an important role in colonial Canada, for their places of business were much more than eating, drinking, and lodging establishments. The innkeeper was often banker, storekeeper, and officer of the court as well as being the host (or hostess, as many widows kept inns after the death of their husbands) to those on the move. The inn was often the first and only enterprise at a crossroads or a clearing and every imaginable activity occurred there as settlers arrived and the community grew. The drawing of lots and distribution of land, political meetings, the sale of land, sessions of court, and government, church services, public entertainment, and militia musters all happened at the local inn.

In the village of Bath, west of Cataraqui on the shore of Lake Ontario, Loyalists Lucretia [Bleecker] and Henry Tinkle had been operating Tinkle's Tavern since their arrival in 1784. They not only served travellers with food and drink but also provided space for court sessions. One of the first trials in Upper Canada was held there when a man was found guilty of stealing a loaf of bread. He was sentenced to thirty-nine lashes, tied to a tree, and punished immediately. It was here, too, that surveyor Asa Danforth made his headquarters while he and his crew were building the first road from Kingston to York in 1799.[9]

Travellers were always concerned with their ability to find a meal as they journeyed to their destination, and housewives learned from the First Nations and developed and shared recipes for simple portable viands to ward off the pangs of hunger. They included Portable Soup, Traveller's Bread, Travelling Lunch, Cornmeal Bread for Travellers, Bannock, Oatcakes, and the staples of the First Nations and the fur traders, Pemmican and Jerky. On the busy but dreadful roads such as Yonge Street, Danforth Road, and Dundas Street, inns sprang up every mile or so to serve the travellers and their horses as they attempted to reach their destinations.

"Peace Be to This House, and to All That Dwell in It"[1]

I N THE years between the creation of the new colony of Upper Canada and the formal declaration of war, there was a steady stream of new arrivals called "Late Loyalists," often from the new republic to the south. They were lured by the glowing reports of relatives and old friends and the abundance of good, accessible land. It was imperative that they become self-sufficient as quickly as possible if they were to survive and prosper despite the climate, the difficulty of transport, and the scarcity of supplies, tools, and equipment.

There were success stories, including that of Hannah Peters Jarvis, daughter of Loyalist Reverend Samuel Peters and wife of William Jarvis, a Loyalist militia officer. When William was appointed provincial secretary and registrar of Upper Canada in 1792, he and his wife sailed on the *Henneken*, arrived in Quebec on June 1, and then proceeded to the capital, Newark, with their three children.[2] Hannah kept copious correspondence, a diary, and a handwritten book of recipes for food, beverages, and medicines between 1792 and 1815, reflective of life in Newark and York. On November 22, 1793, the year after their arrival in Newark, William Jarvis wrote to Samuel Peters, his father-in-law, in England:

> I shall leave my family well provided for. I have a yoke of fatted oxen to come down, 12 small shoats to put into a barrel occasionally which I expect will weigh in from 40 to 60 lbs., about 60 head of dung-hill fowl, 16 fine turkeys, and a doz. Ducks, 2 breeding sows, a milch cow which had a calf in August, which of course will be able to afford her mistress a good supply of milk through the winter. In the root house I have 400 good head of cabbage, and about 60 bushels of potatoes and a sufficiency of excellent turnips.
>
> My cellar is stored with 3 barrels of wine, 2 of cider, 2 of apples (for my darling), and a good stock of butter. My cock-loft contains some of the finest maple sugar I ever beheld, 10,000 lbs. was made in an Indian village near Michellemackinac. We have 150 lbs. of it. It was my intention to send you a small keg of it, but I was taken ill. Also plenty of good flour, cheese, coffee, loaf sugar, etc. In my stable I shall have the ponies and a good slay; the snugest and warmest cottage in the province. Thus you see I shall have the best of companions abundantly supplied with every comfort in the wilderness, where few have an idea only of lonely existing. In fact I am

early provided with every requisite for a long and severe winter which is close on our heels.[3]

The memories of seven-year-old Mary Warren Baldwin, who arrived in 1798 with her family after the hazardous crossing of the Atlantic with the ever-present threat of a shipwreck, were dictated to her daughter, Maria Murney, in 1859, giving us a glimpse of their adventures:

My grandfather and his family reached New York in June 1798.... From Oswego they crossed Lake Ontario to the island — then the peninsula — opposite Toronto, which was then a carrying place of the Indians, and at night they crossed the bay of Toronto, then York, arriving at the celebrated town and finding it composed of about a dozen or so of houses, a dreary dismal place, not even possessing the characteristics of a village. There was no church, schoolhouse or any of the ordinary signs of civilization, but is was in fact a mere settlement. There was not even a Methodist chapel, nor does my mother remember more than one shop. There was no inn, and those travellers who had no friend to go to pitched a tent and lived in that as long as they remained. My grandfather and his family had done so during the journey. The Government House and the Garrison lay about a mile from York, with thick wood between.

After remaining a few days at York the family proceeded to take possession of a farm my grandfather had purchased in the township of Clark [Clarke, in Newcastle District], about 50 miles below York. They travelled in open bateaux, when night came on pitching their tent on the shores of Lake Ontario. The journey generally occupied two days, sometimes much longer. They found on the land a small log hut with a bark roof and a chimney made of sticks and clay, the chinks between the logs stuffed with moss, and only a ladder to go to the loft above.[4]

In 1799, Mary accompanied her father, Robert Baldwin, and elder sister to New York to attend her sister's wedding on February 12, 1800, to a gentleman to whom she became engaged on the voyage to America. Mary did not return to Canada until 1807 and recorded that:

The country had, of course, improved somewhat during the seven years since they went down, still where cities now stand there was then only woods, woods, woods, with here and there a few scattered houses. For instance, at Buffalo, where they passed a night, was a solitary roadside inn, with a swinging sign. No other house, and the beautiful Lake Erie spread out before it.

My mother found York had vastly changed in those years. There were a church, a gaol, a lighthouse building and many nice houses, and the woods between the garrison and town fast disappearing.

My mother went down to the farm after her sisters had returned to New York, and then her experience of "roughing it in the bush" began. The hardships were bearable until the winter came on, which proved to be one of the most severe ever known in Canada.

In the end of the previous summer and the fall, the field mice were a perfect plague. They were found in myriads, and destroyed everything they could find. Everything that was turned up proved to be a homestead destroyed, and the cat loathed mice as the Israelites did quails. The winter made an end of the mice, which lay dead by hundreds of thousands on the ground. But a new trouble arose, very trying to the women and those unable to work. White oak staves were found to be marketable and to bring a large price. Therefore a mania arose for cutting and preparing these staves. Consequently every man in the country set to work at this new employment, leaving the women and old people to get on as they could on their wild lands. My grandfather's man followed the universal example, and they could get no other man for the highest wages that could be offered.

My mother, a young and delicate girl of sixteen, was obliged to drag hay up a hill to feed all the cattle and a flock of sheep, though terrified by the animals, as my grandfather was too infirm to do it himself. There was also a pack of hounds to feed, and water to draw, and logs to draw into the outhouse [woodshed], at which three worked, that is, aunt Alice, my grandfather and mother, and my grandfather chopped the logs in the house to supply the great fireplace, which held what we would call a load of wood almost now.

During the following summer flights of pigeons were remarkable. My mother says they used to darken the air. In December of 1810 the family moved up to York in sleighs.[5]

Robert Baldwin lived with his son, Dr. William Warren Baldwin, until his death in 1816, while Mary married John Breakenridge, a Niagara lawyer in the same year.[6]

The homes that dotted the landscape ranged from humble shelters of canvas, boughs, and bark, to well-constructed dwellings of logs, brick, or stone. They often had appendages of summer kitchens, woodsheds, bake ovens, smokehouses, and driving sheds. A traveller in the early nineteenth century noted: "Many of the houses have a balcony or piazza of wood, erected in front, covered, and floored with the same material. This the inhabitants term a stoop. In such a country it proves very convenient, affording in summer, shade from the sun and in winter, shelter from the storm."[7]

Whether a family was large or small, rich or poor, they would have a central fireplace of stone or brick for warmth, and for cooking food — the heart of the home. If it were only a one-room shelter, there would be straw-filled pallets laid out on the floor for sleeping at night. The space might be divided by blankets, or there might be a ladder to a loft above.

As the family prospered, this first shelter or house often served as the kitchen or summer kitchen to their second or permanent home, or sometimes it was adapted as an outbuilding to store wood or to house small animals or fowl. Becoming established did not diminish the importance of the kitchen and its cooking fireplace.

In these early years in Upper Canada, the proverb "A woman's work is never done" was a fact of life, for whatever her station in life, whether mistress or maid, she bore the final responsibility for the never-ending round of meals and domestic chores needed to survive. Food, beverages, and medicines were required in endless quantities, and very few were ready-made. The wives, mothers, grandmothers, aunts, sisters, and daughters were expected to plant, care for, harvest, dry, or pickle and preserve the fruit, vegetables, and herbs from their gardens, orchards, and fields, as well as salt, smoke, and store wild game, domestic fowl, beef, and pork, while setting aside the tallow and lard to make candles and soap later. It was to the women that an injured or ill family member or neighbour would turn for one of their medicines or advice to relieve distress.

Women needed to be skillful in dairying — milking, churning butter, cheese-making — and in many homes she often needed to know how to brew beer and make wine and other spirits for use at the table or in the sickroom.

To accomplish the daily round and prepare for the long, cold, hard winter ahead, a woman's kitchen, with its cooking fireplace and bake oven, was crucial. Bake stones, bake pots, and earthenware ovens were also used to make the daily scones, rusks, biscuits, bread, and puddings. A woman's tools and equipment included handmade iron and tin utensils such as trivets, long-handled forks, ladles, skimmers, skillets, cauldrons, and pots of various sizes.

The daily round for women demanded expertise with the fireplace, bake oven, and other utensils as they cooked, baked, put up preserves, heated water for cleaning, laundry, and bathing, melted tallow for candles, and performed a multitude of other tasks, as well as made sure three daily meals were on the table for family, friends, neighbours, and servants — breakfast at dawn, dinner at noon, and supper after the chores in the stables and barn were finished in the evening. Before bedtime they were often kneading dough and setting it to rise in a dough box, making or mending clothes, or writing letters to faraway family and friends, all by the light of a fireplace and a flickering candle.

She might be fortunate to own a printed book brought from her homeland, if she was literate, but more often, like Hannah Jarvis, she kept a handwritten book that extended far beyond expectations to include recipes for making dyes, furniture varnish, and different kinds of cement to use for grafting trees, for repairing china, and for mortar to plaster brickwork outside! One of the most useful printed books was *American Cookery* by Amelia Simmons, an American Orphan published in Middletown, Connecticut, in 1796, as she included many ingredients, vegetables, and fruits that did not appear in books from abroad. The first cookbook to be printed in British North America was *The Cook Not Mad or Rational Cookery* by James Macfarlane in Kingston, Upper Canada, in 1831. This was a similar version of a book published in Watertown, New York, in 1830, just thirty-five miles south of Kingston and definitely a North American cookbook with indigenous ingredients that Upper Canadians would have known and used in 1812: turkey, cod, pigeons, cranberries, corn, pumpkins, molasses, pearl ash, and many more!

Every task required preparation — when butter was churned, the milk had to be set until the cream rose to the top and "was on the turn" before churning. Yeast had to be created from potatoes or hops before making bread. There were very few alternatives to using homemade yeast in baking cakes "light" or encouraging pastry to be short and succulent. If a woman did not have homemade yeast, she could beat the batter with a fork, whisk, or fruit tree branch, beat egg whites and add the other ingredients, or add pearl ash. Pearl ash was the more refined version of potash, a by-product of the clearing and burning of the extensive North American forests to establish farms. It is believed that pearl ash was first discovered as a leavening agent by the First Nations, and by the late eighteenth century it was included as an ingredient in Upper Canadian housewives' handwritten recipe books, as well as in *American Cookery 1796* and *The Cook Not Mad*.

The new arrivals in Upper Canada were constantly encountering new food-related experiences — from the First Nations, from their neighbours, and from their harvests of new plants and ingredients that they had not known before. Indian corn, cornmeal, pumpkins, squash, spruce beer, and cranberries were among the ingredients and recipes those pioneer housewives recorded in their own treasured, often tattered handwritten books.

Historic recipes and their sources appear in Chapter 12.

8

"WE PLOUGH THE FIELDS, AND SCATTER THE GOOD SEED ON THE LAND"[1]

A S THE American Revolution ended, we find that there was already significant agricultural development in Upper Canada. The first permanent European farmers in Upper Canada were French, settling at Petite Côte near Fort Detroit. The Pajot family farm near LaSalle is believed to be the oldest farm in the province that has been worked continuously since 1772.[2]

In addition to the fields and gardens cleared and cultivated by both the military and the fur traders surrounding their forts and posts, we learn that there were: seventeen farms with sixty-one head of cattle, thirty sheep, and one hundred and three hogs. On two hundred and thirty-six acres these farms produced two hundred and six bushels of wheat, nine hundred and twenty-one bushels of maize (corn), forty-six bushels of oats, and six hundred and thirty bushels of potatoes.[3]

The flood of Loyalists was to have a profound effect on many aspects of everyday life, including farms and farming. For example, Peter Secord, who had served with Butler's Rangers, crossed the Niagara River, took a six-hundred-acre land and implement grant from King George III, and began clearing twenty-four acres of land on which he raised two hundred bushels of corn, fifteen of wheat, fifty of potatoes, and four of oats.[4] For the most part, the Loyalists were farmers with the experience needed to carve farms out of the wilderness. This flood of farmers was to continue:

Upper Canada had another influx of Loyalists when, in the 1790s, New Brunswick was becoming crowded. Many moved their families again up the St. Lawrence, through Lakes Ontario and Erie, to the Long Point country. They, too, had to get rid of the great forests of beech, maple, white and yellow pine, and walnut to clear fields for crops. One settler describes the daily round as "working from dawn to dark and then walking 3 miles to the river, catching fish by the light of the 'fire jacks,' using the bone of a pike as a hook." The fish, buds and leaves of trees, and milk from one cow brought from New Brunswick kept the family alive until August when a little crop of spring wheat headed out sufficiently to allow a change of diet. The Long Point settlers were not eligible for three years of rations, because this migration was their second, so they all suffered hardships.

All kinds of edible items were consumed — pigweed, lambs quarters, groundnut, and the plant called Indian cabbage. The bark of certain trees was cut in pieces and boiled, as were also the leaves and buds of the maple, beech, and basswood. Occasionally, a deer was shot and divided among the members of the rejoicing community. Frequently, also, great flocks of wild turkeys were seen in the marshy lands, and it did not require an expert shot to bring down the unsuspecting birds. Fish were also easily caught so that as soon as the first year or two had passed the settlers had abundance for themselves and for many strangers "within their gates." Tea was a luxury for many years, with hemlock and sassafras used as substitutes.

Still, a rude plenty existed. As to meat, the creeks and lake supplied fish of several kinds — black and rock bass, perch, carp, mackerel, pickerel, pike, and white fish, and above all speckled trout; the marshes — wild fowl, turkeys, ducks and geese; the woods — pigeons, partridge, quail, squirrels, rabbits, hares and deer. As to other animals in the woods, there were many (too many) wolves, bears, lynx, wild cats, beavers, foxes, martins, minks and weasels. Bustards and cranes also were found by the streams. As to grain, they soon had an abundant supply of Indian corn, wheat, peas, barley, oats, wild rice, and the commoner vegetables.

The ingenious housewives of those times tried to make up for the various articles of food, which they could not produce by the invention of new dishes, and to make the ordinary menu as palatable as possible by some change or addition. One of the most appreciated of the "delicacies" was the pumpkin loaf, which consisted of cornmeal and boiled pumpkin made into a cake and eaten hot with butter. It was generally sweetened with maple sugar.

Another "Dutch dish" was "pot-pie," which consisted of game or fowl cut up into small pieces and baked in a deep dish, with a heavy crust over the meat. On such fare were developed the brawn and muscle, which in a few years changed the wilderness into a veritable Garden of Eden.[5]

The Loyalists included many cultures and religions, and they were soon followed by other organized cultural and religious groups such as Quakers, Pennsylvania Germans, Mennonites, Methodists, Tunkers, French émigrés, Children of Peace, and more.

There were many different ways in which the settler under the British regime could obtain title to land. First in time was the outright grant. The head of each Loyalist family received a clear title to 200 acres and those who had served as officers in British regiments during the American war were given larger allotments. Sons of Loyalists also had the privilege of obtaining land when they were ready to settle on it. Many of these

"United Empire Rights" were never taken up by the original recipient, and became subject to sale or exchange. It is said that on occasions the right for a 200-acre lot might go for 6 pounds, or even a gallon of whiskey!

In Upper Canada, when a new township was opened for settlement, would-be owners would apply for the lot of their choice. The first applicant could pay the nominal fee and take possession, but this was not an outright purchase. It was necessary to comply with certain obligations, such as clearing and tilling a portion of the lot, and erecting some sort of dwelling. Most settlers under this system "proved" their title within a reasonable time, but there were others who purchased for speculation, and who acquired their title by having the work done, or claimed to be done, by others. Later, when surrounding lots had been improved and roads opened, such speculators might expect to sell at a handsome profit.[6]

Swearing an oath of allegiance to the British Crown and turning out for militia training and service were also duties required of landowners.

When war was declared in 1812, it is believed that there were ninety thousand settlers clearing land and raising crops. They were proud of what they had accomplished and looked forward to a future that did not include the war that was to descend on many peaceful communities and farms and destroy them. Elizabeth Russell expressed what many families thought and hoped for:

> We are comfortably settled in our new House and have a nice little Farm about us. We eat our own Mutton and Pork and Poultry. Last year we grew our own Buck wheat and Indian corn and have two Oxen got two cows with their calves with plenty of pigs and a mare and Sheep. We have not made Butter yet but hope soon to do so.[7]

After years of hard work, the men were primarily concerned with the success of their fields and getting their crops ready to be harvested. Beginning with the first meeting of the legislature when they were called to serve, and continuing through the war years, they found "no slight difficulty to be done" in attending the meetings.[8] As one author has told us, "the members of the Legislative Assembly found no slight difficulty in leaving their farms at a season when the crops needed their undivided attention; but sufficient of them gathered together, having travelled in some cases hundreds of miles in canoes and through trackless forests to permit the business of the country to be done."[9]

The crop most commonly sown from the earliest days of settlement was wheat, since it grew readily, and when the seeds were ground, it made excellent flour. Seeds were scattered by hand on the newly ploughed fields and covered by dragging a tree branch or a harrow over them. Harvesting was slow work, usually with a sickle or scythe, raked into rows, gathered into bundles, and tied with a twist of straw. To separate the wheat kernels from the husks and straw, threshing was accomplished by beating it with a flail and tossing the mixture into the air with a blanket. The heavy kernels would fall to the ground while the lighter straw and chaff would be (hopefully) carried off in the wind. According to David Gibson, an early-nineteenth-century farmer and surveyor in York County, some farmers threshed with oxen or horses by making them walk over sheaves laid on the barn floor.[10] To grind the grain into flour, many settlers were forced to use a crude mortar and pestle, while others employed hand-turned querns, one disk-shaped grinding stone rotated on another.

> With abundant water power at hand, it was not long after settlement that full-scale flour mills were set up, using overshot or undershot water wheels. The first such mill in Upper Canada was erected by the government at Cataraqui (Kingston) in 1783. Others soon followed. Farmers brought their wheat to such mills by boat, wagon, or even on their backs. Milling was done on a barter basis, one-twelfth or one-tenth of the grain being left with the miller as payment.[11]

Many mills followed and served the growing population, for we learn that in 1794 the northwest fur trade purchased eighty thousand pounds of flour in Niagara.[12]

Gardens were essential to survival in the settlement years to augment the harvest of wild fruits and nuts as well as the grain and root vegetables usually grown in the fields. A plot was typically chosen close to the house where the soil was fertile and rich, or on a southern slope to trap the early-morning sunlight and take advantage of the short growing season. The planting and care of the garden that contained herbs and vegetables were usually the responsibility of the women and children, and the harvest of root vegetables was stored for the winter months in barrels of sand, sawdust, or bran in a cool, dry place. Some vegetables were pickled in vinegar, while fruits were preserved in syrup made of sugar, honey, molasses, maple syrup, or spirits. Herbs and slices of apples or pumpkins were hung to dry near the fireplace and then stored in clean cotton bags or crocks safe from rodents.

Upper Canadian farm families became keen observers as they watched the sky, streams, forests, and fields during the changing seasons. They learned to be flexible, to compromise, and to adapt as nature bestowed and withdrew the blessings they hoped for. When war arrived on their farms, this skill was put to good use to ensure their families survived.

9

WHEN ONE DOOR SHUTS ANOTHER OPENS[1]

L AND WAS the lure that brought ever-increasing numbers of newcomers to Upper Canada in the late eighteenth and early nineteenth centuries. Whether professional, craftsman, or farmer, they wanted to own land, since it would be their fortune and a legacy for their children. These newcomers wanted and needed services just as the fur traders and military had, and this sparked the growth of the tiny communities that had already sprouted around the forts and posts. It also led to many new communities wherever two roads intersected or a stream provided the power that could be harnessed to run a mill.

In addition to all those already discussed here, a brief introduction to a few of the many organized groups that arrived in Upper Canada illustrates how very different they were, despite their common purpose.

The Loyalist settlements in what would become Glengarry County attracted Scottish Highlanders at the end of the eighteenth and beginning of the nineteenth centuries as the economy worsened "at home." When lots were drawn originally, each township was assigned to a Scottish corps, and comrades who wanted to be neighbours traded lots to accomplish this. Many of the men became prominent in the North West Company fur trade, and after years of service, they returned to retirement on their land close to the two great rivers they knew so well and had travelled so often.

When the French Revolution ended, supporters of the Royalists found themselves in dire difficulties, and it is believed that thirty thousand fled to England where £9 million was provided to support them. England could not sustain this assistance and looked to alternatives, including granting settlement lands to Comte Joseph de Puisage and about forty Royalist followers in Upper Canada. The site for their settlement was finally confirmed between York and Lake Simcoe on lands surveyed north of Markham, Pickering, and Whitby in addition to twenty-two lots of two hundred acres each near Bond's Lake on Yonge Street, where a town called Windham was to be established.

While the new arrivals struggled to clear their land, they lived in temporary barracks until they could build log houses. Their leader, de Puisage, visited Niagara, bought a three-hundred-acre farm for $3,000, and rebuilt and refurnished the house that commanded a beautiful view of the Niagara River. He took his housekeeper, Mrs. Smithers, and his two servants, Marchand and John Thompson, with him, leaving his friends and colleagues to the challenges they were ill-prepared to solve.

Alas, the new settlement north of York did not fare well, for the toil, privation, and hardship overwhelmed the newcomers, and as they received patents to their land, many sold and returned home.[2] However, there were some success stories, such as that of Madame Vallière, who was still keeping a wayside hostelry at Big Creek Bridge (later Heron's Bridge, Hogg's Hollow, and York Mills) with help from her son and grandson when war was declared in 1812.

When the French Royalists' land was put up for sale, who was buying? In most cases it was Laurent Quetton St. George, one of de Puisage's group, who was determined to adopt the new country as his own. Upon arriving, Quetton St. George spent his last $10 on a peddler's pack to enable him to trade with the First Nations and the settlers. He soon owned about twenty-six thousand acres of the settlement, and by 1802 had not only opened a trading post at the Narrows of Lakes Simcoe and Couchiching to barter with the First Nations, but had posted this advertisement in the *Niagara Herald*:

New store, at the house of the French General, between Niagara and Queenston.

Messrs. Quetton St. George & Co. acquaint the Public that they have lately arrived from New York with a general assortment of Dry Goods and Groceries, which will be sold at the lowest price for ready money, for from the uncertainty of their residing any time in these parts, they cannot open accounts with any person. Will also be found at the same store, an assortment of tools for all mechanics. They likewise have well made trunks and empty barrels.[3]

With rare foresight, Quetton St. George not only travelled to Lakes Simcoe and Couchiching to trade with the Mississaugas but also established stores at Amherstburg, Kingston, Lundy's Lane, and York, in addition to Niagara. In 1803 he was advertising "liqours, spices, butter, cheese, chestnuts, hickory, black walnuts & cranberries," and cautioning his customers that "nothing, however, will be received in payment but cash, bills of exchange or furs."[4]

Transport was a serious problem, and a few months later Quetton St. George announced that "he is sorry — he has not received his East India goods and groceries. He is sure they are at Oswego, and should they not arrive this season, they may be looked for in the early Spring."[5]

Despite the setbacks, his stock continued to expand and his business grew. His advertisement on February 20, 1808, is invaluable, because it is an extensive list of seeds available in the pioneer outpost of York: "red onion, white onion, green marrowfat peas, blood beet, early cabbage, winter cabbage, savoy cabbage, red cabbage, scarcity, lettuce, cucumber, early cucumber, turnip, sage, carrot, parsnep [sic], radish, french turnips, summer squash, winter squash, watermelon, musk melon, early beans, early purple beans, asparagus, summer sabory [savory] celery, parsley, pepper grass, burnet, caraway, pink."[6]

Thomas Talbot was born in 1771 at Malahide Castle, Ireland, and entered active service in the 24th Regiment at Quebec when he was nineteen years old. When Colonel Simcoe arrived, Talbot joined his staff and travelled with him as he explored Upper Canada. Talbot was impressed by the wild, untamed beauty of the north coast of Lake Erie. Eight years later, on Christmas Day 1800, he surprised the fashionable English society to which he had returned when he announced he was selling his commission and going back to Upper Canada. By 1803 he had acquired five thousand acres on the north shore of Lake Erie and was developing a vast settlement bearing his name. Talbot ensured that roads were surveyed and openly encouraged settlers. He built his own home, which he named Malahide Castle after his birthplace, halfway between the Niagara and Detroit frontiers. This was an excellent location for several gristmills and sawmills, which became prime targets for the Americans during the war.

Another large and very successful group of settlers were Pennsylvania Germans. They had pioneered and farmed in pre-revolution United States but now sought new homes and fertile land among friends.

The ancestors of these people were originally from the Palatine, a German province on the upper Rhine generally influenced by Martin Luther. After the seventeenth century war between the Catholics and Protestants, 40,000 Palatines left the country in search of civil and religious liberty. Many went to London, where Queen Anne offered them a home in Pennsylvania or along the Mohawk Valley in New York State. Here, under British rule, they were joined by thousands of other Palatines from their homeland. By the time the American Revolution broke out in 1776, the original pioneer farms were comparable to those they had left on the Rhine in 1709. By the 1790s, many were becoming disturbed by the Anglo-American settlers' influx into their territory. William Berczy's migration from the Genessee Valley in New York State to Markham was the greatest influence in their coming to Upper Canada. Beginning in 1798 and streaming along until 1805, the solemn trek to a new country moved on, night and day. The covered wagons were drawn by oxen with a few cattle walking behind, making about eight miles a day for 500 miles, along the Allegheny River, around Lake Erie, across Niagara, bound for Upper Canada.[7]

The Pennsylvania Germans travelled in groups of ten or twelve families, and as well as their farming knowledge, many were trained craftsmen and crafts-women: "Three things cannot be over-emphasized in considering these people; they were physically equipped both in knowledge of what to do in the wilderness and the strength to do it; they came with money and equip-ment; and they aided one another, whether Quaker,

Huguenot, Lutheran, or Mennonite. Religious or racial differences meant little in a community."[8] They settled in three geographical areas: Niagara, north of the town of York in York County, and in Waterloo County, contributing their skills to the neighbouring villages and towns.

Daniel Tiers, a Pennsylvania German bachelor, settled about 1794 in William Berczy's German settlement in Markham, later moved to York, and turned his hand to chair-making. On January 23, 1802, he advertised in the *Upper Canada Gazette*:

> The Subscriber returns his sincere thanks to his Friends and the Public for the great encouragement he has hitherto met with, and begs leave to inform them, that he now intends carrying on his business in all its branches without delay — armed chairs, Sittees, and dinning ditto, fan-back and brace-back Chairs. He very shortly expects a quantity of different paints; it will then be in his power to finish his Chairs in the best manner, and by his great attention to perform his promises, hopes to merit protection and support.
>
> N.B. He also expects a quantity of common Chairs from below [Lower Canada], which he will dispose of on reasonable terms.[9]

After little success in the chair-making business, Tiers opened the Beef-Steak and Beer House in York in 1808. A short time later he launched the Red Lion Hotel at the corner of Yonge and Bloor Streets, which became the starting point for the Yonge Street stage coaches.[10] In August 1812, Tiers was cited in the *York Gazette* for "his prompt and spirited Excertions in apprehending *two interesting Personages* who eloped from Bed and Board alias the Common Gaol [jail] on Wednesday last."[11]

Tiers was among the leading York merchants to form the York Association on September 22 "for the purpose of issuing Bills for the purpose of making change" to fight the coin shortage plaguing Upper Canada in 1813.[12] A stroll along King Street would have confirmed that many merchants had joined Tiers and

> opened a shop while others had set aside a room in their house to serve the public. The most popular was Ms. Lumsden's Confectionary where, in addition to peppermint pastilles, sugar sticks, marzipan figures and other treats, she offered a wide range of gingerbread hearts, fishes, ponies, parrots and dogs.[13]

Customers could also visit the baker John Horton and examine his smoked beef, sundry articles of groceries, bread and cakes, perhaps choosing a fine seed cake to take home. Three other men, Mr. Rock, a hairdresser, and Evans Eveans, a tailor and habit maker, both from London, as well as Elisha Purdey, a watchmaker, were all new arrivals, in addition to the general store, six taverns, and other artisans showing steady development and growth in the new capital.[14]

Although York had a late start compared to the earlier communities, once it was designated the capital (even on a temporary basis), there was a flurry of activity to not only equal its rivals but to surpass them. Prior to the war, York had passed a Stump Act, and prisoners in the jail had to work off their sentences by clearing the streets of tree stumps. The pound keeper was kept busy rounding up the animals running loose as he attempted to capture the hogs, sheep, oxen, cows, and horses and holding them in the large new pound until their owners claimed them.

At the eastern edge of the community stood the first brick buildings intended to be the wings of a large central structure. These Parliament Buildings were constructed of local clay and were home to meetings of the legislature, sessions of the court, church services, and other social activities. The nearby rivers provided power for three gristmills: the King's Mill on the Humber River and Skinner's Gristmill on the Don River. There were also three sawmills on the Don, one owned by Skinner and the other by Paschal Terry, while Cooper's Grist and Sawmill was located on the Humber. Two potash establishments were active: Duke Kendricks's on Yonge Street and William Allan's opposite the jail. This by-product of land-clearing and log-burning was in demand as an export for soap-making in England, so it was important to York's economy.

A market had opened on Saturdays in 1803 to serve the "Farmers and Settlers in the Town and Township of

York and the several adjacent Townships, exposing pub-
licly for Sale, Cattle, Sheep, Poultry, and other Provisions,
Goods and Merchandize brought by Merchants, Farmers
and others."[15]

On the eve of war, York was a small, but growing town with a population consisting mainly
of artisans, labourers and transient farmers.
Merchants, civil servants and government officials were divided by their intense rivalry and
by differences of outlook and background, however they were united in their opinion of their
own importance, and brought on York the envy
and opprobrium of the rest of the province.[16]

10

....

DESPERATE DISEASES MUST HAVE DESPERATE REMEDIES[1]

From THE beginning of time, men and women have searched for treatments of the ills of body, mind, and spirit. Historians have observed: "The dog hunts the fields for his special grass medicine; the bear dresses the wound of her cub or fellow-bear with perhaps as much intelligence as primitive man observes in his empirical practice. Primitive man does not know why his medicines work; he simply knows that it does cure."[2]

When newcomers arrived in British North America, they brought with them a limited knowledge of medical practices carried out at that period by doctors, surgeons, and dentists who often had little or no formal training. The newcomers were far more familiar with the beliefs, superstitions, herbal remedies, cures, and preventive measures they had learned from their families and neighbours and practised since childhood. They often brought seeds to plant in their new herb gardens near the door to their homes and began to learn from the First Nations the value of the wild vegetation that surrounded them.

The new arrivals would have heard the often repeated story of that famous explorer Jacques Cartier, who in the winter of 1535–36 turned to the Huron Domagaia, recently cured of scurvy thanks to Native knowledge of plants, to save his crew from certain death. The curative powers of a broth and a poultice made from the bark and needles of *anneda* (possibly white cedar), which are rich in the vitamin C needed to cure scurvy, was used and became a Canadian legend.[3]

It was from the writings of the early explorers, missionaries, fur traders, soldiers, and entrepreneurs that records emerged and were preserved describing Native traditions, beliefs, and remedies. Many of them were, and are, based on a "doctrine of signatures" and the belief that plants exhibit visible signs of their use. For example, wild strawberries, shaped like a human heart, will strengthen or cure a patient with heart problems. Plantain was named by the Natives "white man's foot" because of the shape of the leaves and their recognition that it arrived with the white settlers and followed them wherever they travelled. The leaves were soaked in warm water and applied as dressings to wounds, or wrapped around aching feet to relieve the pain and fatigue of long hikes, while wet tobacco was a favourite remedy for bee stings.[4]

Ginseng would have been known to the newcomers, since it was a treasured plant in their homelands. Imported from China at great expense and thought to be a panacea for all manner of medical difficulties and diseases, it often achieved seemingly miracle cures. The root, in the shape of a man, was particularly valuable, they believed. They must have been surprised and pleased to find it growing in the moist soil of the hardwood forests in Upper and Lower Canada. The First Nations called it *ginens* and employed it as a stimulant and to ease stomach pains and bronchial disorders as well as to alleviate headaches, fevers, asthma, and nausea. As well as using it as a medicine, the Natives believed it was a potent love potion or charm.[5]

The spikenard, a member of the ginseng family, was a favourite remedy for wounds, prepared by making a salve from the berries or roots. It could also be mixed with wild ginger as a poultice for treating bone fractures and wounds, or to relieve inflamed areas of the body.[6]

Colds, coughs, fevers, influenza, and ague (probably malaria) were common complaints that plagued the newcomers, and a number of decoctions were made to treat these maladies. Usually the plant parts were gathered in advance, then dried and stored in clean cotton bags, ready for boiling or steeping in water. When needed, the patient could be given a full cup or more of the remedy. A few of the most common plants included the tops and leaves of boneset to reduce fever, relieve body pains, and treat colds; sarsaparilla roots for coughs; the inner bark of many types of willow to reduce fevers; and the inner bark of the native evergreen hemlock to relieve influenza-like symptoms.[7]

With the newcomers, beliefs about the medicinal powers of "spirits" arrived, as well:

Alcohol, it was thought, kept out heat in summer and cold in winter, supplied strength to labour, helped digestion, warded off disease, and did many other marvellous things. Many people believed, contrary to scientific reality, that alcohol gave warmth in the cold northern climate of these colonies. It was also supposed to have great medicinal value. "In many families, whisky was served to each member of the household in the morning," one writer recalled. "It was considered to be a precaution against colds and to enable one to do hardy work." Taken straight or mixed with various herbs, alcohol was a regular household remedy for many health problems, often in the form of patent medicines. A popular remedy for cholera, for example, was Huxhams Tincture, which contained two ounces of Peruvian bark, a half-ounce of Virginia snake root, and three and a half pints of whisky. In keeping with this custom, whisky consumption allegedly rose during the cholera epidemic of the early 1830s. Doctors were more likely to prescribe brandy and wine as stimulants and tonics.[8]

There were few doctors in Upper Canada at this period, and those who did live in the colony were usually attached to military regiments. Scottish-born doctor Robert Kerr arrived in 1776 and served as surgeon to the King's Royal Regiment of New York. Later he lived in Kingston and Newark where he served the Indian Department, conducted a private practice, and married Elizabeth, the daughter of Molly Brant and Sir William Johnson. Like the other medical men, he played an important role in community life as a supporter and subscriber of the new Presbyterian Church and the Masonic Lodges in the Town of Newark. The Statement of Losses during the War of 1812 confirms the success of those early gardens and orchards as well as Kerr's dependency as a doctor on some plants for the making of medicines:

A garden with every sort of fruit Trees, four Vineyards, and a large nursery of grafted and inoculated Fruit trees of all Descriptions; (Cut down by order of Lt Philpots of the Royal Engineers). The best garden in the province; to which every Gentleman in the district will Certify. £250.0.0.

A List of Fruit Trees etc in Robert Kerr's Garden — Almonds, Apricots two sorts, Plumbs six sorts, nectarines two sorts, Cherries four sorts, Peaches Eleven Sorts, Pears five sorts, Apples twelve sorts, Currants three sorts, seven sorts of Gooseberries, Strawberries three sorts, Rasp-berries, four Vineyards, Flowers & Medicinal Plants, Flowering Shrubs, and Ornamental Trees.[9]

Dr. William Dunlop was born in Greenock, Scotland, in 1792 and arrived with the 89th Regiment of Foot in Canada in 1813 from the army depot on the Isle of Wight. He served as a surgeon at Fort Wellington, attended the wounded from the Battle of Crysler's Farm, and later served at Gananoque, Kingston, York, and Fort George. Dunlop was also at the siege of Fort Erie and took part in the Battle of Lundy's Lane. It was in the latter that he went into the firing line and carried several men on his back to the safety of the hospital quarters where he could treat them.[10] During the winter of 1814, Dunlop led a company of Canadian Fencibles and some militia in the construction of the Penetanguishene Road to link York to a new naval base planned on Penetanguishene Bay for the defence of the Upper Lakes: "Working under incredible hardship, with snow six feet deep, without horses and oxen, the men laboured on the road throughout the winter. The snow was so deep that a pit had to be shovelled around each tree in order to give the men room to swing their axes."[11]

This remarkable doctor was known as "Tiger" Dunlop because of an encounter in India where he met a tiger and threw snuff in its face to escape its attack. When the war ended, Dunlop was asked by the government to act as an agent for the settlers making claims for the losses suffered during the conflict. The red-haired and bearded giant also became the warden of the woods and forests for the newly formed Canada Company and was a legend in his own lifetime.

The doctors at this time had little knowledge, training, or understanding of the challenges they were facing concerning the ills of the human body and used bloodletting, puking, and purging as standard practices, often adding to their patients' suffering and in some instances causing death. They used many drugs, both botanical and metallic, including mercury, antimony (a brittle silvery-white metallic element), and calomel, which was considered to be a great cure-all. When Dr. Solomon Jones, a Loyalist physician in Augusta in eastern Upper Canada, ordered medical shipments from Montreal, they included calomel, corrosive sublimate of mercury, opium, laudanum, terebinth (turpentine), aloes, castor oil, and powdered cantharides.[12]

With so few doctors available, in most communities and homes it was the women who were expected to have on hand the ingredients and the "receipts" for making medicines for illness and accidents. In some cases they were committed to memory, while in others they were handwritten in their journals. Elizabeth Simcoe recorded on many occasions her ill health and the simple remedies she used: "I was feverish & felt great relief from a Saline drought taken in the effervescent state, a little salt of wormwood water & two teaspoonfuls of Lemon juice. Cat mint in the tea is a good stomatic & sweet marjoram tea for the headache." While out for a walk she described what she learned about the plants around her:

> Ginseng, a root which the Merchants tell me
> they send to England & in some years has sold

at a guinea a pound, Sarsaparilla — Golden thread — the roots look like gold thread. When steeped in brandy they make a fine aromatic tincture & liquorice plant; consumption vine, a pretty Creeper. Green's daughter was cured of a consumption by drinking tea made of it. Poison vine in appearance much like the former but differs in the number of leaves, one has 5, the other 7. Madder, toothache plant, a beautiful species of fern, Sore Throat weed, Dragon's blood, Adam & Eve or ivy blade, very large, which heals Cuts or burns, droppings of beach, enchanter's nightshade, Dewberrys Wild Turnip which cures a cough — it is like an Arum.[13]

Fifteen years later, and hundreds of miles away, Lydia Bacon recorded the accident that injured and blinded her husband on October 1, 1811, and the simple remedies that restored his eyesight and good health:

Josiah has been burnt with gun powder, which might have destroyed life had not a kind Providence prevented. He was priming his gun, for the sake of shooting some wild fowl which are plenty on the river. The flint of the gun being rather long, struck fire into the powder, in the pan by coming in contact with it in shutting. The flask, which contained nearly half a pound of powder exploded, throwing the contents into his face, burning his eyebrows and lashes close. He shrieked, and putting his hands to his face took the skin entirely off. He could not see at all for a fortnight, and we sometimes feared that he never would see again. But a simple curd made of new milk and vinegar cured his eyes, and an application of oil and brandy alternately applied to his face healed it rapidly.[14]

Handwritten and printed cookery books contained instructions for medicines, salves, and potions for many family ailments, including those of Hannah Jarvis:

Sting of a Bee or Wasp
A young Onion — applied raw —

Ague
1 oz. — cream Tartar — 1 oz Sulphar — 1 oz Cloves — 1 oz Bark — 3 half pints molasses — a table spoonful taken hourly till all is gone.[15]

For many women, childbirth was a dangerous experience, while for others, such as Hannah, who wrote to her father, Samuel Peters, on December 5, 1792, shortly after she delivered "that she had never been so well, not having had a single pain after delivery." In every community it was hoped there would be a midwife who was an older woman who had acquired some experience attending a large number of births. If a midwife was not available, the expectant mothers relied on their female family members or neighbours. These dedicated women were willing and able to respond at any hour of the day or night to the rap on their doors by anxious men seeking assistance for their wives, mothers, sisters, or daughters. They, too, were the unsung heroines of the early nineteenth century.

11

....

KNOWLEDGE IS POWER[1]

LIFE IN the settlements in Upper Canada was not for the faint-hearted. To survive and prosper took a combination of experience, skill, and knowledge, no matter what one's station in life might have been.

A sound knowledge of the land, the seasons, animal husbandry, and the economy were just a few of the attributes needed by farmers or yeomen and their families. The craftsmen or women who wanted to open a small shop or business and serve their customers needed to be experts in their trades whether as a blacksmith or dressmaker. Many had served apprenticeships as long as seven years to learn their crafts or trades and had apprentices serving them. Merchants, millers, innkeepers, distillers, and other businessmen and women needed the financial resources to become established and to allow their customers to have credit until crops were harvested or allow debts to be paid with "any kind of produce from their farms or gardens."

For many professionals such as doctors, dentists, chemists, lawyers, clergymen, teachers, surveyors, or engineers, training was usually acquired before they arrived and their knowledge was much in demand in the growing villages and towns. The Legislative Assembly drew on established landowners, businessmen, and professionals to serve as magistrates, Members of Parliament, and other powerful offices because of their education.

Formal education in Upper Canada was virtually unknown, since there were very few organized schools during this period. The Loyalists were accustomed to community schools open to all children, while some authorities held the European ideas of the time and believed formal education was for the children of the elite, those with social rank or financial means. Scottish settlers wanted education for all, while other cultural groups stressed that their children were needed at home to help with farm work or to learn a craft or trade as apprentices.

The Executive Council of Upper Canada recommended the establishment of grammar schools in Cornwall, Kingston, Newark, and Sandwich in 1798, but it was not until after the passing of the Grammar School Act in 1807 that eight schools were actually founded, one school in each district of Upper Canada. The act also assured an annual salary of £100 per year for a schoolmaster in each school.[2]

In many communities it was the boys or young men who attended the small private local schools held in homes, or in a public building such as the local church. The first school may have been at Cataraqui (Kingston) as early as 1785. The first rural school in Upper Canada was opened in Fredericksburg in 1786 by John Clarke, followed by Mr. Smith in Ernestown a few months later, Mr. Lyons in Adolphustown in 1789, and by D.A. Atkins in Napanee in 1791.[3]

In York the best-known and possibly earliest school was William Cooper's from 1798 to 1801. Cooper, from Bath, England, had many other talents and enterprises, as well, including auctioneer, tavern keeper of the Toronto Coffee House, and reading prayers on Sunday. Later, in 1806, he built a gristmill and sawmill on the Humber River. Cooper was licensed to teach in 1799 and focused on reading, writing, arithmetic, and grammar.[4]

When Reverend George Okill Stuart was nominated Anglican minister at York in 1800, he took a few students to augment his meagre income and he, too, concentrated on the basic four subjects.[5] By 1801 a log school was built in the tiny community of Newtonbrook on Yonge Street north of York. As so little of the forests surrounding the farms was cleared, these early schoolhouses were built on the road or path, otherwise parents worried that their children might get lost or attacked by wild animals.[6]

John Strachan, born in Aberdeen on April 12, 1778, and educated there, began life as a teacher. In 1797

> he received the offer, through Hon. Richard Cartwright and Robert Hamilton, to proceed to Canada to organize and take charge of a college, which Governor Simcoe had determined to establish at York, the seat of government in Upper Canada. Unfortunately, when the young

Scotchman arrived in Canada in the winter of
1799, Governor Simcoe had left the Province,
and the scheme was, for the time, dropped.
Mr. Strachan, much disappointed, remained in
Kingston as tutor to Mr. Cartwright's children.[7]

Strachan remained in Upper Canada, eventually entered the Church of England, and was ordained
in 1804. Like many other clergymen, he began taking
students, gradually developing the famous Cornwall
Grammar School. Many young gentlemen travelled
to attend it, including Jonathan, the eldest son of Dr.
Solomon Jones of Augusta, George and Thomas Ridout,
Samuel Jarvis from York, and William Grant from
Kingston.[8] Strachan's students were often influential
in public affairs in the later years, among them Chief
Justice Robinson, the Honourable J.B. Macaulay, the
Honourable Jonas Jones, and the Honourable Archibald
McLean.[9] When Strachan accepted the vacancy at the
church in York in 1811, he again carried out his dual
professions of preacher and teacher.

There were other alternatives by now as classes were
offered in taverns, at a writing school, and at an evening school for the benefit of young female (or male)
apprentices. Fees were to be paid with a combination of
currency, candles, and firewood.[10] On the eve of war, the
first recorded school in Ontario County was opened in
1811 in Whitby and conducted by a Miss Cross.[11]

The declaration of war wreaked havoc on the struggling school system as teachers such as John Langstaff,

who had been conducting classes in Markham Township, went off to war in 1812 to keep the books for the quartermaster's stores. The coming of peace found many of the tiny log buildings in appalling conditions, but often still used for community events. Reverend John Strachan, who had arrived in York in the late summer of 1812, was a tower of strength for the citizens during the wars years and was much in demand when it ended to visit homes and settlements in the surrounding area. Strachan accepted the invitation of Seneca Ketchum to travel north on Yonge Street to Heron's Bridge (later known as York Mills) to conduct a service and recalled it many times:

> It was the month of November 1815 and the day happened to be rainy and cold, and roads at the same time, bad. The appointment to conduct a service at 3 o'clock nevertheless was kept, but to his great mortification, no preparation whatever had been made…. The schoolhouse was in a ruinous state. It had no chimney, but merely a large hole in the roof through which the smoke might escape where there happened to be any fire, and the furniture consisted of a short school form, a table and a broken chair. The audience consisted of two persons, and the rain pelted on their heads through the roof. The service nevertheless was gone through and a sermon preached with the same care and solemnity as if hundreds had been present, and that in the most finished, sacred edifice …[12]

The war was over before the introduction of the Common School Act in 1816 that was meant to bring some stability and standards to providing a modest education for the children. It may have been responsible for the decision to build the first school in Uxbridge, where both school and schoolmaster were remembered by Joseph Gould:

> Until I was about ten years old, there was no school in the township; nor was there any nigher than the Quaker schoolhouse on Yonge Street, almost twenty miles west of our place. In 1817 or '18, a log schoolhouse was built on the north-west corner of lot 31, in the 6th concession. A little Irishman was employed to teach the school. But the teacher was like the house, a poor one. I had been taught the alphabet by my mother [Rachel Lee, a Quaker] before I went to school, and was able to spell and read a little.... The people were all poor, and poor was the school, they could only keep it open for three or four months during the winter season. I got a smattering of the three R's there, and such was the extent of my schooling.[13]

12

"Strange to See How a Good Dinner and Feasting Reconciles Everybody"[1]

I N THE years leading up to the declaration of war by the United States, every housewife, housekeeper, or cook in a military or fur trader's kitchen was limited by the climate, short growing season, limited technology, lack of ingredients, and poor transportation. Everyone developed gardens — military personnel, fur traders, doctors, merchants, settlers — and the rich virgin soil of Upper Canada produced harvests beyond expectations. The challenge was the lack of good roads and reliable, safe transport to move produce, supplies, and ingredients to markets.

The First Nations had adapted to their surroundings, its blessings and its shortcomings, for they could be on the move to better hunting, fishing, or gathering locations, but the newcomers seldom had that freedom. They were all attuned to their surroundings and what nature might provide. Foraging in the wild for food was part of everyday life, and once war was declared the settlers realized that nothing was safe from either the invading or defending armies, something we will learn more about in upcoming chapters. In the meantime, what follows are some examples of fresh tastes from the wild and gardens for reliable everyday fare.

Dandelion Greens

They can be used until they bloom. Pick over carefully, wash in salt water, and rinse in several waters. Put in boiling water with a piece of salt pork. Boil one hour. Drain well, add salt, and boil another two hours. When well done and tender, turn into colander and drain.[2]

Dandelion roots were and are an excellent substitute for coffee. They should be gathered in fall or early spring. Wash thoroughly without removing the brown skin. Cut into small pieces and roast in a slow oven until crisp and dark brown. Grind the pieces and store tightly covered in a cool place.

Dandelion Wine

Five quarts of dandelion flowers,* two gallons boiling water; let stand overnight; in morning strain, add five pounds sugar, six lemons, boil one hour, take off and strain into a stone jar and let it stand two or three weeks, add half pint whisky and strain into bottles. Good for spring medicines.
*Always pick the dandelions on a sunny day.[3]

As summer and fall brought other gifts of edible plants as well as fish and game, they were gratefully harvested and the surplus was preserved for the winter months by drying, smoking, salting, or packing in sand, sawdust, or bran. Food could also be preserved with sweeteners such as maple syrup or sugar, honey, or molasses, as well as pickled with salt and vinegar. Sauerkraut was a favourite dish of the Pennsylvania Germans who arrived in Upper Canada in the late eighteenth and early nineteenth centuries. It was also an excellent source of vitamin C and was often carried on vessels to prevent scurvy on long voyages.

Sauerkraut

10 lbs. cabbage
¼ lb. salt

Shred cabbage, and put alternate layers of cabbage and salt in a clean stoneware crock. Press each layer, until juice rises to cover cabbage. Lay cabbage leaves on top, cover with a plate, and hold down with a stone. Store in a cool place. Make sure cabbage is always covered with liquid and add salted water if necessary. Ready to eat in six weeks. Eat raw whenever possible.[4]

Gardens were developed as soon as land could be cleared, and not only raising the produce but preserving it was a priority.

There was much bartering and trading among the First Nations, the military, the fur traders, and the settlers. However, this was an era of few ready-made ingredients or foods, thus long hours were spent by everyone who was cooking or baking "starting from scratch" before a meal was prepared.

Bread has not only been called "the staff of life," but was the foundation of meals for both the First Nations and newcomers. For centuries the First Nations made bannock or twists of dough on sticks over a fire or by frying with cornmeal, ground chestnuts or walnuts, and fat and water. The newcomers brought wheat or oats to plant as their grain of choice, and when they could not reach a gristmill to have their grain ground into flour, they improvised with hand-turned querns or pounded their harvest in a mortar and pestle. Simple unleavened combinations of flour or meal and water were baked over open fires, in bake pots, brick ovens, or on griddles (or girdles), including bannock, biscuits, and scones. Leavening agents were scarce or unknown in those years unless the cook or baker made their own yeast from potatoes or hops or a combination of the two. A crock or bowl of homemade liquid yeast (often called "emptins") covered with a towel would be kept in the larder, or the kitchen so a quantity of "old" yeast was always available to add to the new supply. The following recipe was handwritten by Hannah Jarvis in her cookery book and was in use in Upper Canada in 1811:

Potato Yeast — Excellent

One pound of potatoes peeled — boil them
nearly dry — then beat till smooth — when still
warm add tablespoon brown sugar one of yeast
— let stand 24 hours — when it will be fit for
use — by keeping a little and adding as above
you will have a constant supply.[5]

Almost a century later printed Canadian cookery
books were still carrying recipes for the baker or the
cook wanting to make their own yeast.

Rusks were a well-known, small, light loaf, twist,
coil, or roll of bread in the late eighteenth and early
nineteenth centuries often eaten at breakfast:

Rusks

One tumbler milk, I teacup of yeast, 3 cups
flour, 3 eggs made into a batter overnight in the
morning add a coffee bowl of sugar butter the
size of an egg, flour sufficiently thick to mould,
then butter your dishes, fill them set them near
the fire, when light cover them full with white
of egg and sugar.[6]

For cake or cookie-making, or any other fine, light
baking, yeast was not always suitable and other measures were tried as mentioned in Chapter 7: beating air

into the batter for long periods of time (often as long as two hours!), beating egg whites and adding to the batter, or adding pearl ash. When pearl ash was added to batter or dough, it quickly produced carbon dioxide and appeared to work like magic. Lydia Bacon recorded in her diary on May 17, 1812, that she had a large bag containing a number of necessities, including "a huge sponge cake presented by a friend on the morning of our departure."[7] The cake was then four days old, for she had left Vincennes on May 14, and it would have been baked a day previous to their departure from a traditional recipe that depends on the beaten egg whites to make a light cake.

Sponge Cake

8 eggs, the weight of them in sugar, the weight of 4 in flour, nutmeg to your taste — Beat the yolks & sugar together, then add the whites & flour —[8]

In comparison, in *The Cook Not Mad*, we find pearl ash listed in a rare cookie recipe, for cookies were newcomers at this period to Upper Canadian kitchens:

Nice Cookies That Will Keep Good Three Months

Nine cups flour, three and a half of butter, five of sugar, large coffee cup of water, with a heaping teaspoonful of pearl ash dissolved, in it; rub your butter and sugar into the flour, great spoonful of caraway.[9]

The housewife or cook needed to know how to read but also how to cook and bake to use these printed books, for they seldom contained directions for mixing or oven heat, but were simply a list of ingredients.

Because of the difficulty of transport and availability of ingredients, every family, community, fort, and post attempted to be as self-sufficient as possible. Gardens, fields, nearby streams, and forests yielded many foods, while livestock such as pigs and cattle and domestic fowl such as chickens, ducks, and geese added to the larder. The milk that could be turned into butter and cheese, plus the eggs to be gathered daily for consumption and baking, were a bonus. Some of the dairy products were also used for medicines and for their healing properties, as well. Earlier, in Chapter 10, we discovered how Josiah Bacon was cured of a very serious injury to his face and eyes with milk, vinegar, brandy, and oil.

Hearty soups and stews were the mainstays for many meals, for a huge cooking pot could simmer over the fire either indoors or outdoors, or on the back of a stove for hours while other tasks were performed. The following recipe for a hearty stew was eaten by Barracks Master John Askin and his family at Fort Michilimackinac in the late eighteenth century. Askin was also a merchant and had a Native servant named Charlotte who served as the cook in their home.

A Michilimackinac Stew

2 pounds beef
½ cup Indian corn
½ cup peas
4 medium potatoes
2 tablespoons flour

Debone and dice beef. Brown meat thoroughly.
Peel and dice potatoes. Place beef, potatoes, and
peas in pot and cover with water. Dissolve flour
in 1 cup water and add to pot. Allow to simmer
until gravy begins to thicken. Add corn and
continue to cook at least 20 minutes or longer.[10]

A similar stew was made daily by the soldiers at Fort
Niagara during the British years. Easy to prepare, with
the ingredients at hand, it could be varied in many ways.

Ration Stew

1 pound salt pork
½ pound dried peas or rice
fresh or dried vegetables

Brown the salt pork and cook in pot of water for
½ hour. If peas are used soak in water until they
swell. If using rice add directly to boiling water.
Fresh or dried vegetables can be added later as

well as herbs from the fort's garden as flavouring. Simmer until done, about 2 to 3 hours.[11]

Newcomers to British North America brought their
centuries' old love of puddings with them and were surprised to find that the First Nations had also been making
a pudding-like dish for centuries. Cornmeal was the
original basic ingredient, and over the years it became
known by many names — Indian Pudding, Canadian
Pudding, and Grandmother's Pudding.

Indian Corn Flour Pudding

2 ounces Indian corn flour
½ pint milk
¾ pint boiling milk
1 egg
sweetening and flavouring to taste

Mix the corn flour smooth in the cold milk, and
then stir in the boiling milk. Add sweetening
and flavouring if desired (vanilla is most appropriate). Put into clean stewpan and stir over the
fire until it becomes thick; beat in the egg, put
the pudding in a buttered dish and bake in a
slow oven for about an hour.[12]

Puddings could be savoury or sweet, used to stretch
a meal, or to comprise the whole meal. They could be

made of any combination of flour or stale flour products such as bread or biscuits mixed with chopped vegetables, meat, fruit, seasonings, and fat. The plum pudding may have been introduced to Great Britain by the conquering Danes in 1013 as a broth that developed over the centuries into a thickened pottage or porridge. Finally, in the eighteenth century, when pudding cloths were used for the increasingly popular batter puddings, pudding took on a solid form and shape. In British North America, potatoes and carrots were often substituted for the scarce dried fruit, and it was then called Carrot Pudding. Carrots contained sugar, which lessened the need for a sweetener.

Tea would have been the most popular beverage for women, while beer that could be made in your own kitchen with ingredients from the nearby forests and fields, would have been a favourite of the men:

Spruce Beer

8 gallons water
1 gallon molasses
1 gill of spruce*
3 pints good yeast
a small quantity of potash when bottled
*gill = quarter of a pint or a half cup
spruce = spruce boughs boiled in water until it tastes of spruce

Put in a clean crock. Shake well together. Let it stand a week to work. If the weather is warm it will take less time. When drawn off to bottle, add spoonful of molasses to a bottle.[13]

FIRST LETTER FROM MARTHA

Big Creek Bridge
(soon to be Heron's Bridge)
Yonge Street
Upper Canada
June 4, 1812

My dear Mary,

When I check my diary and find the date of my last letter to you, I am ashamed that my pen has been idle so long, and I hope you will forgive me.

I was not able to take up my duties as mistress at the school here and was kindly offered lodging by a good French innkeeper, Mrs. Vallière. It soon became apparent that I must find other employment, and Mrs. Vallière suggested that I assist her until the future of the school is known. I agreed, and we are so busy here at the inn night and day that I scarcely have a minute to myself. We are just six miles from the capital York on the busiest road in the area, and we never refuse visitors a bed or a meal. If we are over-full, the hay loft is used for the men folk, and the women and girls share the rooms indoors. We are well situated here beside the farm, as we have a barn with a large stable, driving sheds, a big garden, two good wells, and two brick ovens for bread and baking. Madame Vallière, a widow, is the owner and manages it well. She is a fine lady and her son, James, and her grandson, Bill, are both hard workers.

This road was once just a path used by the Native people and the fur traders, but now is wider and stretches from York north to Lake Simcoe. Some of the stumps and roots have been removed, but when it rains the bridges are washed out. A river called the Don crosses the road here, and the hills on both sides are so steep the road winds off course to use the more gradual slopes. Many of our countrymen are employed by the North West fur-trading company here and gave some money to help fix this road so they can use it to reach their posts in the northwest.

They now paddle their very large canoes up the Don River from the bay on Lake Ontario and here winch them up the steep hill on the north and put them on wheels to Holland Landing and then by water through Lake Simcoe, the Severn River, Georgian Bay to Michilimackinac.

Many of the settlers here at Big Bridge are countrymen, too, and what are called here Loyalists as they lived first in the colonies to the south and had to flee when the revolution broke out — Kendrick has a potashery on his farm, Humberstone is a potter, and the van Nostrands, Harrisons and Willsons are farmers. Samuel Heron has moved to our valley, late of York where he had business problems, and has now built two mills — one for sawing and one for grinding. There are rumours he plans to open an inn here, too, because there is so much need for beds, food, and drink. There is also a rumour the name of our settlement will be changed to Heron's Bridge soon, so when you write to me next, put both names on my letter, lest it go astray.

You asked what I do here for my mistress and I scarce know where to begin, as the days are never the same.

Today was a very busy and special day, for the militia mustered here as they always do on King George's birthday. Knowing that, I mixed, kneaded, and set extra bread to rise in our bread box beside the fireplace last night. The flour is made from our own wheat and ground at Heron's Mill, and the yeast is from our own hops. I asked the lads to chop more wood and draw extra buckets of water in readiness for cooking and washing up today.

We had a family of eleven who stopped last night at the inn with their two teams of horses in our stables. They are on their way to their land near Thornhill, and I knew I must be up early for their breakfast today. I made the oatmeal porridge last night as we always did at home and set it near the fireplace, and I set the table, too. This morning I warmed the porridge quickly and poured pitchers of rich cream for it. While they ate it, I quickly cut slices of ham to fry along with two dozen eggs, and many slices of stale bread to toast over the fire and eat with our churned butter. As soon as the kettle boiled, I made two pots of strong tea from the new box we bought in York last week. They seemed much pleased, and as Bill had fed and harnessed their horses, they were soon on their way northward.

As soon as we all had our breakfast, I washed up, brought my dough to the bake board, kneaded it down, shaped loaves, and put them to rise again in the dough box. I tidied the bedrooms, emptied the slops, fired up the outdoor bake ovens, and helped my mistress with dinner for the militia that were gathering outside for their drills. By now the boys had milked our cows, filled the wood box, and topped up the pile beside the outdoor ovens.

My mistress decided on stew for dinner, as we had some dried beef in the larder as well as some garden vegetables packed in barrels of sand from our harvest last fall. She hoped that with a brisk boiling, lots of new fresh herbs added from this year's garden, and a rich gravy, along with our freshly baked bread and butter, we would have a tasty dish. Between cutting, peeling, and chopping I put my loaves in the oven, and they turned out well today as it was a fine sunny day. We have trouble here with our ovens on damp, cold, and rainy days.

What to have as a sweet for dinner was a question until we remembered our pie plants had many tall, rosy shoots, probably enough to make several puddings. Quickly, we pulled the biggest shoots, cut off the roots, and let them fall in the patch, then cut off the leaves to clean our pewter with later. I washed the stems and cut them into small pieces while my mistress prepared some of Mr. Humberstone's shallow basins for baking by rubbing with butter and mixing some butter, maple sugar, and flour to make a topping to cover the fruit. We have heard that some folks call this plant rhubarb, but in this house it is called pie plant because womenfolk round about here use so much of it for pies.

Forty-two men and boys washed up at the horse trough and then sat down to dinner. There were great bowls of beef and vegetable stew, crocks of our homemade pickles that kept good over the winter, bread and butter, pie plant pudding, apple cider, dandelion wine, tea, and spirits for some of the older men.

There was much talk at the tables of war and rumours of war, but everyone is hoping for the best, even as the boys play their fifes and drums and the men, young and old, practise marching and musket shooting this one day of the year.

I, too, hope for the best with the school reopening so that I can do the work I love so well. In the meantime I must do my best for the mistress here, for business is good and if we are to prosper we must look to our fields and garden, keep our larder well stocked, and our barroom and spirit and wine cellar well supplied with genuine articles. We know that our neighbours, whether farmers, millers, craftsmen, and all, think the same way and trust in God to keep us safe.

It has been a long day and I must go to my bed, but I pray you will write soon.

Your loving sister,
Martha

13

"THE FIRST BLOW IS HALF THE BATTLE!"[1]

WE MAY never know what flashed through Captain Charles Roberts's mind when he received word from Major-General Brock that war had been declared by the United States. It was July 8, 1812, and this was indeed confirmation that swift action was needed.

Captain Roberts as commander at Fort St. Joseph must certainly have been among those "who were hoping for the best while preparing for the worst" in the years and months leading up to that day.

How did Brock, and in turn Roberts, know so quickly that President James Madison had signed a declaration of war against Great Britain on June 18? The web of human relationships that had developed in Upper Canada and beyond was the key, for everyone involved in the fur trade was vitally interested in the possibility of war lest their valuable cargos of furs and trade goods that were moving throughout the Great Lakes and the St. Lawrence River were seized by the Americans. Many of the Montreal merchants had business contacts in New York, and on hearing of Madison's declaration they sent dispatches to Canada. When Brock received the news at York, he in turn sent messages immediately to the western posts.

Why the western posts and this isolated one in particular? The answer rested in its location and value. It was in a strategic position to take advantage of the fur trade and to keep the loyalty of the First Nations. As commander, Roberts knew not only of the value of controlling this place but also the long and checkered history of the area, for it had been home to both fur traders and military posts for close to a century. The original post was constructed by the French Army in 1715 and sheltered and protected Jesuit priests as they conducted their missionary activities with the First Nations. It also served as a base for fur traders such as Jean-Baptiste Rousseau, who had a fur trade licence in 1778 to barter with Natives.[2] Following its defeat at the Plains of Abraham in 1759, France ceded its land and holdings in North America to Britain, which took possession two years later. The British military was soon followed by North West Company traders prepared to take over the abandoned French commerce in the area.

In 1781 the British feared an American attack as part of the Revolutionary War strategies and decided to move the fort to Mackinac Island, seven miles away. Lieutenant Governor Patrick Sinclair began the laborious job of relocating buildings and salvageable materials to the island. Once established, British soldiers destroyed the remnants of the original fort so that the American rebels could not use it.

Alas, the Treaty of Versailles in 1783 meant another move for the British fort to the north shore of Lake Huron. St. Joseph Island was chosen and both the military and North West Company relocated, with the company developing a canoe-building post, a blacksmith shop, and other permanent services for its trade. By 1796 the British flag was waving over the community that had developed on the island and the north shore of the St. Mary's River. A canal had been constructed to circumvent the rapids in the river, allowing small craft laden with furs or trade goods to travel easily between Lakes Superior and Huron.

This was a difficult posting, over three hundred miles and three months of travel to Amherstburg, with commanders and regiments always looking for another rotation. Some commanders had imported livestock and developed gardens that servants tended. Junior officers often lived outside the fortress in houses rented from absentee fur traders, while others resided in the fort and had their meals provided by a military kitchen. The enlisted men lived in the barracks in the fort, and Lieutenant Landmann described their weekly rations of four pounds of salt pork, three pints of dried peas, six ounces of butter, six ounces of rice, and seven pounds of flour for making bread.[3] They were allowed to hunt and fish and brought in rabbits, pheasants, partridge, and other small game as well as pike, bass, and trout to augment their rations. The enlisted men were also given land for gardens plots and attempted to raise vegetables despite the chaotic weather. An example that everyone remembered and recounted was that Lieutenant Landmann arrived on June 3, 1800, in scorching heat and the next morning six inches of snow covered the ground![4]

Roberts must have realized that he had no time to lose. He knew Fort Michilimackinac well, knew that it was stronger than his fort, knew that Lieutenant Porter Hanks of the U.S. Artillery had a larger force of sixty regulars to his thirty-nine men. After all, had they not watched out for each other's deserters through the years and escorted them back to the garrison where they belonged? Had they not supplied each other with provisions in times of need? Five years ago they had loaned the American fort twenty barrels of pork when it was in short supply.[5]

Captain Roberts realized that if he acted at once he might capture Fort Mackinac before the Americans knew that war had been declared. The First Nations, the fur traders, French Canadians, and North West Company employees responded to his appeal for support for his small force. As a result, he led six hundred men who sailed in the North West Company's schooner *Caledonia* and a flotilla of canoes under the cover of darkness on July 17 and landed at 3:00 a.m. on Mackinac Island. They brought two British cannon with them, and when they landed, local farmer Michael Dousman gave them a yoke of oxen to pull the artillery to a hill overlooking the fort.[6] Lieutenant Porter Hanks did not know that war had been declared and had no alternative but to surrender.

Thus, the web of human relations that had been forming for years — military, fur traders, First Nations, farmers, and Métis — had, without loss of life or drop of blood, seemingly managed to create a miracle.

"I Have a Large Bag on the Pommel of My Saddle"[1]

On May 17, 1812, Lydia Bacon, the twenty-six-year-old wife of Lieutenant Josiah Bacon, quartermaster of the 4th Regiment of the U.S. Infantry, rode north to Detroit, which she had heard was "gay and dissipated." Lydia was the eldest child of Levi and Mary Stetson of Boston, and in 1807 she had married Josiah, not only a resident of her native city but for years her school companion and playmate. Soon after their marriage, Josiah entered the American army as a commissioned officer.

Lydia had accompanied her husband for over a year as she, along with many other officers and enlisted men's wives and children, followed the regiment led by Colonel John P. Boyd. She had already travelled from her hometown of Boston to Philadelphia, to the village of Pittsburgh, en route to the village of Vincennes in Indiana Territory. They reached Vincennes on October 1, 1811, with many observations recorded about everyday life in the new republic:

August 8th. ... We stopped this evening at a beautiful place without a name, and took a pleasant walk along the bank. We are in the habit of buying butter, eggs, &c., as we go along, and have found them abundant, cheap and good. Needing some butter now, we called at a house hoping to have our wants supplied; but the good housewife very carelessly told us that she had been making *soap* that day, and not having sufficient grease had supplied the deficiency with butter. What a country, thought I, where people can afford to use sweet butter for soap grease![2]

September 4th. ... Last night we had a *recruit* added to our number, in the shape of a bit of female mortality born in a tent on the banks of the Wabash, which river we are now ascending.[3]

October 5th. ... The troops have left for Vincennes to-day. It was a sad sight to see them depart for war. A number of fine young men, volunteers from Ohio and Kentucky, left their studies in college to participate in this campaign.[4]

As Josiah had injured his eyes, he did not leave until a few days later. Lydia and the other officers' wives stayed in a boarding house, and Lydia described their situation as:

... very much exposed, while the troops were absent, for every body left that could handle a sword or carry a musket, and we women remained without even a guard. Mrs. W. and myself had loaded pistols at our bedside, but I very much doubt whether we should have had presence of mind enough to use them, had we found it necessary. If the Indians had been aware of our situation, a few of them could have burnt the village, and massacred the inhabitants. But a kind of Providence watched over us, and kept us from so dreadful a fate.[5]

By the end of November, Josiah, "after being exposed to that most horrid of all battles — an Indian attack," was "preserved in safety."[6] With the returning officers and men, Lydia learned of the losses and heartbreak in her first encounter with the reality of war:

Lieutenant Peters relates an affecting incident of this battle. Among the militia from Kentucky was a Captain Spencer who had been in *twelve* Indian campaigns. He was accompanied in this expedition by his son, an intelligent boy about twelve years of age. This brave little fellow had a gun adapted to his size, went on guard in his turn, and fought like a man. During the fight the darkness prevented any one from knowing who had fallen. Each feared for his fellow. As soon as the fight was over, this poor boy sought

his father, but alas! he was not among the living — the hero of so many battles had at last
met his fate. And a gentleman searching for his
friends found this afflicted child weeping over
the mangled body of his father. My heart aches
for him, and for his distressed mother, who is
left poor, with a large family of children to be
supported by her own exertions. Alas! many
others are made widows and orphans by this
dreadful fight. Oh, when will brother cease to
lift his hand against his brother, and nations
learn war no more![7]

This was the Battle of Tippecanoe, as Lydia named
it in her journal. In time, many historians realized that
it was the first battle of the War of 1812, although it
occurred before war was actually declared. In early
March 1812, Lydia had a new experience and recorded:

We visited what is called a sugar-camp last
week, and were much gratified with witnessing
the process of sugar-making. This part of the
country abounds in sugar-maples. Large trees
are selected in which holes are bored and tubes
inserted. These tubes convey the liquor which
runs from the trees into a trough prepared for
its reception. It is very clear, and pleasant to the
taste. This is boiled in large kettles, or caldrons;
and when sufficiently done (which those who
make it seem intuitively to know), it is made

into sugar by being constantly stirred while cooling. This article is most delicious, as all who have tasted it will testify. The labor of making it here is performed by blacks, superintended *by their mistress*. The lady whom we saw doing it in this instance, was a person of great respectability and abundant wealth. I enjoyed my ride to the sugar-camp very much. It was a beautiful afternoon; the air was mild and sweet, the weather delightful, and my pony upon whose back I rode, stepped along with a springy gait which seemed to say that he enjoyed it too.

This climate is so mild that I have put on no extra clothing this winter except when walking or riding. And then a large shawl was sufficient even in the coldest days. Only a very little snow has fallen, and this disappeared as soon as it touched the ground. Trees bloomed in February, and the gardens are now quite forward. Lettuce, radishes and asparagus we have already, and this without the assistance of hot-beds.[8]

By the end of March, they received orders to proceed to Detroit and also learned of the mode of travel:

The troops are *to go by land*, and not *by water*, as was at first thought. The distance from Vincennes to Detroit by the route we are to take is six hundred miles, and we are to sleep on the ground in tents. It will take some days to accomplish this journey. We are to proceed to Newport, Kentucky, from thence cross the river to Cincinnati, and go through Ohio to Michigan. We shall pass through some thriving villages, but mostly through woods and prairies, where none but the hunter and the Indian have penetrated. The journey looks formidable in prospect. Mrs. F, Mrs. G and myself are to ride on horseback. My husband being on the staff, will have the same privilege. So I shall be spared the distress of seeing him encounter the hardships which those who march must necessarily endure. I have been learning to ride on horseback, and like it much; but how I shall succeed in going through swamps and fording rivers, experience alone will determine.[9]

Lydia fared much better than the soldiers' wives, for she had obviously become a competent rider, and on May 17 and 19 she recorded:

I have a large bag hanging to the pommel of my saddle, containing necessaries. Among other things, I have a Bible and Homer's Iliad (translated) for the mind, while for the stomach, provision is made in the form of a huge sponge cake presented by a friend on the morning of our departure.

My feelings to-day have been much tried by seeing the poor soldiers' wives trudging along on foot, almost knee-deep in mud, and some of them with a little child in their arms. Only four or five wagons are allowed to carry the baggage, and of course the poor women must suffer. I should think it would kill them. We passed two houses to-day which were deserted by the inhabitants through fear of Indians. We understand that a camp of them is near us on a hunting excursion. Our friends express the fear that we may suffer for want of good food. Surely they might spare such concern for *me* if they would only remember that *I* have *the very best Bacon* in the world! Mother, you would laugh to see our cook roast chickens. He takes a green stick, and placing the fowl upon one end sticks the other in the ground before a good fire, and biddy roasts to a charm. Or, if a joint of meat is to be cooked, two sticks are put in the ground with their tops shaped like a fork, so that another stick can rest across them. From the last stick the meat is suspended in the centre and cooks very well indeed. We have a pack-horse who carries a pair of mess-boxes for our accommodation. These boxes are made with separate apartments, which hold our cups, plates, &c. Our tea is carried in cannisters; our table is the hind-board of a wagon set on a portable cricket shutting up like a cot bedstead. Our candlestick is a bayonet with the point in the ground, the part in which the gun fits serving admirably for a socket to put the candle in.

P.M. To-night we have encamped near a house. The landlady is very patriotic and gave the soldiers a generous supply of milk.[10]

Their progress through Kentucky and Ohio was a triumphal one because of their feat at Tippecanoe:

May 29th. ... As we pass through Kentucky great respect is paid to our regiment. It is amusing to see what a parade they make over us. One old gentleman asked one of the officers "if those young women, (meaning Mrs. F and myself,) came all the way from Vincennes?" He was told that we did and that one of us had been the whole campaign! This answer filled him with wonder and admiration. We have passed through Frankfort, another flourishing town in Kentucky. The inhabitants treated us with every possible attention, giving a dinner both to the officers and soldiers. And when we were leaving the town a salute was fired, accompanied with three cheers.

June 10th. We crossed the Ohio, at Cincinnati, at two o'clock this afternoon. The boats which were sent to convey the troops across the river were ornamented with the American and regimental colors. Two companies of Artillery waited on the bank to receive us. They fired a salute, and then escorted us through an arch erected for the occasion, on which was inscribed "To the Heroes of Tippecanoe." When the troops reached the encamping ground a handsome collation awaited them, which had been prepared by the hospitality of the people of this delightful town. The officers and their ladies had been previously invited to General G's, where we were entertained with an elegant and liberal hospitality.

June 12th. We have at last reached Urbana, where we found General Hull with fifteen hundred militia waiting for our regiment. We were received with great respect some distance from the town, and escorted into Urbana through an arch ornamented with oak branches and laurel from the forest. In the centre of this arch the American eagle spread her broad pinions, while on one side of it was inscribed "Tippecanoe," and on the other "Glory." We take up the line of march tomorrow for Detroit. A party precedes us to cut roads and make them passable. General Hull and Governor Meigs, of Ohio, called on the Ladies of the regiment immediately on our arrival. These gentlemen are both very courtly in their manners, particularly General Hull, who is Commander-in-Chief to the troops.[11]

By July 1, the soldiers had reached Michigan Territory, and after they passed through the small village of Miami, it was now thought best to send the baggage, together with the sick and feeble, *by water* to Detroit, while the army performed the remainder of the journey by land. A small unarmed vessel had been sent from Detroit for this purpose, and in this Mrs. G, Mrs. F, and myself embarked. Being much fatigued with riding six hundred miles on horseback, and sleeping fifty nights upon the ground, we thought the change would be pleasant. So we left the army in fine spirits, anticipating the pleasure which we should enjoy in resting, and expecting to reach Detroit in a few hours.[12]

Their enjoyment was short-lived, however. When they were within eighteen miles of Detroit, opposite the village of Malden on the Canadian side, they were intercepted and boarded by an English captain and his men. It was only then that they learned that war had been declared:

Our captor was an English captain, by the name of Rulet, and a very gentlemanly young man. He took the helm, and our vessel was in a very short time anchored at Malden, and we prisoners to his majesty, George III. This was an honor I had little anticipated, and one moreover, that I could very willingly have dispensed with. However, there was nothing but to make the best of it. The English quarter-master soon came on board.

Lieutenant Gooding introduced the ladies to him, observing that we were all officers' wives. He assured us that we should be treated as such, and invited us to his own quarters until we could procure accommodations at the public house. So Lieut. G and his wife, with Mrs. F and myself, went home with the quarter-master. We were introduced to his wife, whom we thought a very pleasant lady, and were handsomely treated to cake and refreshments, so that for a few moments we almost forgot our real situation.

A number of Indians were at Malden, several of whom were engaged in the battle of Tippecanoe. Hearing that it was some of the 4th regiment who were taken prisoners, they followed us through the streets to the public house, scowling upon us with faces truly terrific. After dinner several British officers called upon us. Finding them disposed to be civil and friendly, I took courage to request them *to allow Mrs. F and myself to proceed next day to Detroit.* They very courteously granted my request, pleasantly adding, "We do not make war upon the ladies." Lieut. Gooding could not be paroled, and of course his wife chose to stay with him. That night we slept on board *a prison-ship,* but as we were the first prisoners who had been placed there, it was clean and comparatively comfortable. We slept very well, considering the novelty of our position. I awoke early in the morning, having a strong desire to set my feet on *republican ground* ere our national anniversary arrived. Tomorrow would be the 4th of July![13]

A chaise and driver for the passengers as well as a cart to transport their baggage were provided, and soon Lydia, Mrs. F, two small boys, sons of militia officers, and a soldier's wife with her infant in her arms were happily jogging toward the ferry landing and the vessel that would take them across the river to what they presumed would be the safety of Detroit. When they arrived, the ladies were conducted to General Hull's headquarters where they were

most cordially received by his daughter-in-law, the wife of Captain H. who was keeping house for her father. The rest of the family, excepting this only son, were in New England. With this lady I tarried while in Detroit, and received all the attention and kindness which a refined mind and generous heart could bestow. She had two dear little girls, and the care which they required, together with their pretty and endearing ways helped to relieve much of the tediousness of our unpleasant situation. For from this time the continual din of war caused us sleepless nights and anxious days. No Sabbath and no sanctuary privileges blest us with their return. All days were alike employed in preparation for brother to shed his brother's blood. A war with England seems most *unnatural* — 'tis like a family taking up arms against its own. But if we are forced to do it our cause is just. And I trust that the same kind Providence who fought for us in the Revolution will still succor and protect this highly favored people.[14]

Now that General Hull knew that war had been declared, he crossed the Detroit River and occupied the village of Sandwich. Hull's men camped on Colonel James (Jacques) Bâby's farm, and the general moved into the colonel's "beautiful mansion." Major-General Isaac Brock, who had been preoccupied in York with meetings of the legislature, assembled his troops, met with the First Nations on the Grand River, rallied the militia, and set off for Amherstburg on August 7. Hull retreated back to Detroit and sent a force to escort a supply and cattle train coming from Ohio.[15] On August 15, Lydia recorded:

A summons has been sent to-day, from General Brock (the British commander in Canada,) to General Hull, demanding the surrender of Detroit and the army to the English! This our general has not seen fit to comply with. Every preparation is now making for a bombardment. The British soldiers are very busy in pulling down the large house which conceals the battery which they have been so industriously con-structing. If I were not so terrified at the idea of a siege, I could laugh to see their hurry. Never did a building come down faster in a raging fire than in the hands of these bloodthirsty fellows. The women and children are to go into the fort as the only place of security against the savage Indians, and the bombs, shells, and shot of the English. The officers who came with the summons have left us to return, and as soon as they arrive upon the opposite shore, the firing will commence.[16]

Lydia took Mrs. H's three-year-old and hustled to the fort to take shelter. Before long the British cannons began firing on Detroit and continued until well after midnight. The ending of the bombardment allowed some of the women and children seeking protection in the fort to finally get some sleep. Lydia told of some of the civilians with her in the fort: "Capt. B, an officer in the company, had two days previously to the commencement of hostilities married a sweet little girl of fourteen years! She was with us, having under her care a little nephew, a child five years old. The two hand in hand, like the 'Babes in the Wood,' cried themselves to sleep."[17]

The next morning the bombardment resumed at dawn:

The enemy had got the range of the fort so completely that it was now judged unsafe for the women and children to remain any longer in it. So we were all hurried to the root-house, which was on the opposite side of the fort, and was bomb proof. Never shall I forget my sensations as I crossed the parade ground to gain this place of safety. You must recollect, dear mother, that my feelings had been under constant excitement for many weeks, and now were wrought up to the highest pitch. Complain I *would* not, weep I *could* not; but it seemed as if my heart would burst. My hair stood erect upon my head, (which in the hurry of escape was uncovered,) as I raised my eyes and caught a glimpse of the bombs, shells, and balls which were flying in all directions. The boy warrior, whose father was killed at Tippecanoe, was running about upon the parapet exposed to the fire of the enemy, and seemed as fearless as if in sportive play. On going into the root-house I found it nearly full of women and children....

... the enemy effected a landing on our side, under cover of their armed vessels. Of these they had a sufficiency to demolish Detroit if they chose, while we had not a boat in order to carry a single gun. General Brock's effective force was also double ours, and the Indians were now let loose on the inhabitants. In addition to this our supply of provisions and ammunition was extremely small, and a part of General H's most efficient troops were at this juncture at some distance from Detroit, having been sent away on duty a short time previous to the summons to surrender. Under these circumstances General H, after consultation with Colonel Miller, thought it best to capitulate, and obtained the best terms he could. A white flag was accordingly displayed upon the parapet as a signal for the cessation of hostilities. Immediately the cannon ceased to roar, and all was still. General Brock then sent to ascertain for what purpose the white flag was displayed, and learned the determination of the General H to surrender.[18]

Brock and Tecumseh met for the first time in Amherstburg and immediately recognized in each other the strength of character needed to succeed. They convinced Hull that their forces were enormous so that the American general not only surrendered the fort but also the supply and cattle train that was en route to Detroit.

Our soldiers were then marched on to the parade ground in the fort, where they stacked their arms, which were then delivered to the enemy. The American stars and stripes were then lowered from the flag-staff, and replaced with English colors. A royal salute was now fired with the very cannon which the Americans had taken from the British in the Revolutionary war, and their music played their national tune, "God save the King." How shall I tell you our grief and mortification at this triumph of our foes. A thousand emotions struggled in my breast, too numerous for utterance, too exquisitely painful to be described!

The poor fellows who were shot in this contest were all buried in one grave....

August 19th. The prisoners were put on board his Majesty's vessels to-day. They are to be sent to Niagara and from thence to Montreal, on their way to Quebec. Thus a second time in the short space of six weeks am I a prisoner. I fear I shall not be so easily released this time, as my husband is with me; and a man is of more consequence to the enemy as a prisoner than a woman. Whether my husband obtains a parole or not, one thing is certain: I shall not leave him unless I am compelled to. We were put on board the Queen Charlotte, a fine armed vessel of three hundred tons. In the same ship were General Hull and son, a number of Fourth Regiment men, both officers and soldiers, together with several public civil officers from Detroit. There were only three ladies, Mrs. Fuller, Mrs. S, the young bride of fourteen, and myself....

We were fourteen days out before we reached Buffalo. Eleven of these were spent in waiting for a fair wind, and we were only three days actually sailing across the lake. We landed at Fort Erie, nearly opposite Buffalo, on the Canada side. Here the British commanding officer gave

General Hull liberty to fill the carriage which had been provided for him and his aid, (and which was the only one which could be procured in the place,) as he pleased. My husband had been acquainted with the General and I had boarded in his family, which I suppose was the reason why he offered *us* the vacant seats in preference to others. Officers of the line were obliged to be with their men; but as my husband's duties ceased when the soldiers became prisoners, he could avail himself of the comfortable conveyance ...

... at five in the afternoon we arrived at Newark. This is a very pleasant village directly opposite Fort Niagara. Here we found good quarters, and soon discovered that they were the very rooms which were occupied by Lieut. G and wife ere he was ordered into closer confinement. It was quite a pleasure to me to find their names traced upon the wall. But we were not detained at Newark long. Very providentially for us Gen. Brock was at this place, on his way to Montreal. At General Hull's request he gave my husband his parole *because his wife was with him....*

My dear Josiah having received his parole was most anxious to depart. Accordingly the next day we left King George's dominions with heartfelt joy. *We had but twenty-five cents with which to travel five hundred miles*, the troops not having received any pay for a long time. The communication with Detroit being so hazardous the money had not been sent....

The river which divides Newark from Niagara is there quite narrow, and in a few moments we were safely landed in *our beloved United States.* We breathed a *mental hurra!* and imagined our respiration freer. Oh, liberty! country! home! ye are magic words, and dear to every uncorrupted human heart!

We went immediately to the fort, escorted by our brother officers, who saw our boat approaching and came to the wharf to receive us....

But being naturally most anxious to see our dear parents and relatives, we proceeded the next day on our journey towards dear New England. My husband had obtained funds for this purpose from the paymaster at Niagara. At this time the stage coach did not run farther than Buffalo, which was about thirty-six miles from Niagara. So we hired *a cart*, which was the best vehicle the times afforded. In this we put our trunk, and spreading a mattress over it made us as comfortable a seat as circumstances would allow. But the roads were dreadful, being most of the way made of logs slightly covered with earth. We bore the jolting until our limbs were almost dislocated, and then resorted to walking as a relief.[19]

As the journey back to Boston continued, they were able to take the stage and found at every place they stopped Josiah had to answer innumerable questions respecting the surrender of Detroit from officers stationed all along the road, as they had only heard imperfect reports. At ten o'clock in the evening Lydia and Josiah finally arrived at home in Boston after seventeen months and "were received by my dear mother and sisters with open arms and a shout of joy."[20]

Thus ends the remarkable record of Lydia Bacon's travels and the challenges she met and conquered during 1811 and 1812 in her homeland and in Upper Canada. Lydia's careful recording of meetings with "enemy officers" and their care and attention to her safety and well-being gives the reader rare insights into the calibre of British military and Canadian militia training of the period. For Lydia's journal to have survived is nothing short of a miracle, and for that we must be grateful to the archivists librarians, historians, and custodians who have cared for it for close to two centuries.

15

"A WELL-REGULATED MILITIA IS OF THE UTMOST IMPORTANCE"[1]

IN A speech opening the Upper Canada Legislature on July 28, 1812, Major-General Brock said the following with regard to the Upper Canadian militia and the preparations for war: "Our Militia have heard that voice and have obeyed it, they have evinced by the promptitude and Loyalty of their Conduct, that they are worthy of the King whom they serve, and of the Constitution which they enjoy."[2]

In reality the militia was a particular challenge for Brock, and in his personal correspondence he questioned whether the militia would be of use during the inevitable American invasion. In theory every able-bodied man in Upper Canada between the ages of sixteen and sixty was part of the militia, which could present a very impressive body of men for the defence of the province; in practice the militia were under-armed, under-trained, and unenthusiastic. They lacked virtually everything: weapons, ammunition, uniforms, tents, blankets, food, even boots and cooking pots.[3] Brock and his generals also needed to balance their need for the militia in the defence of Upper Canada with the necessity to plant and harvest the crops required to sustain the citizenry and military. When war was declared in June 1812 and the militia was mustered, the world turned upside down for residents of Upper Canada who were part of the militia. No longer were their militia duties limited to a few days of training per year; they were expected to take up their arms and go to war.

The Militia Act of 1793 detailed the military obligation of residents of Upper Canada with numerous amendments and supplementary acts passed as required. With the increased threat to Upper Canada from the United States, the 1808 provisions commanded every male inhabitant between the ages of sixteen and sixty who was capable of bearing arms to enrol in the militia company in his home district. Exemptions were made for Quakers, Mennonites, and Tunkers, whose objections to bearing arms were respected. However, they were required to register with the treasurer of their districts and pay a fine of 20 shillings in peacetime and £5 in wartime for this exemption. Exemptions were also made for

> judges of the King's Bench, the clergy, the members of the legislative and executive councils and their respective officers, the members of the House of Assembly and its respective officers, the civil officers of the province (attorney general, solicitor general, and so on), magistrates, sheriffs, coroners, half-pay officers, militia officers

who had held a commission in any of the King's dominions and had not been cashiered, the surveyor general and his deputies, seafaring men actually employed in the line of their calling, physicians, surgeons, masters of public schools, ferrymen, and one miller to every grist mill.[4]

The typical militia regiment consisted of eight to ten companies composed of no more than fifty and no less than twenty privates. Some regiments also included drummers and fifers. Officers for the regiment — a major, lieutenant-colonel, and colonel — were appointed to the regiment from the leading gentlemen of the colony. The higher the social status, the higher the rank was. Because the militia was organized by county, as the population of a county increased, a second regiment would be created with more officers commissioned and companies established.[5]

Each militia's commanding officer was responsible for mustering the regiment for training. Often the training coincided with King George's birthday on June 4. The musters contained some attempts at military training such as marching and field manoeuvres, shooting contests with a hat as a prize, and general orders being read. However, most were an excuse for a day away from their chores, a free meal and drinks at the local inn or tavern, or a chance to learn the latest news and gossip and enjoy the muster's festive atmosphere. Some commanding officers provided the regiment with barrels of whisky to toast King George's health; many members toasted the king's health more than once, often leading to a muster ending in drunkenness and a brawl.[6]

Brock's largest complaint against militias was their apparent lack of enthusiasm for the war. Despite what Brock said in his speech to the assembly on July 28, 1812, he privately complained that he was unable to "animate the militia to a proper sense of duty."[7] Two main factors played into the militia's lack of enthusiasm for the war: first, the flood of recent immigrants from the United States, and second, the time spent on duty and away from their farms or businesses was placing their livelihoods and therefore their families at risk.

A large number of the recent settlers to Upper Canada were immigrants from the United States who had little or no strong loyalty to the British Crown. These recent immigrants were passively pro-American, as opposed to the Loyalist immigrants fleeing from the revolution a few years earlier. Many of them declared that they were still Americans and should be considered neutral in the conflict and could not be forced to fight against their American friends and families. Brock attempted to have an oath of abjuration added to the Militia Act, forcing militia members to pledge allegiance to the king and foreswear any loyalty to a foreign power, but the bill never passed in the legislature.[8] Michael Smith, an American Baptist preacher in Upper Canada at the time, suggested that the representatives voted against the bill based on their constituents' wishes and that if the bill had passed there would have been a rebellion by American settlers.[9]

When war was declared in June 1812, the idea of being mustered and sent away from home was very difficult for many men to accept. They were not opposed to defending their homes and property but were reluctant to report to garrison forts on the other side of the colony. The men had crops or businesses to attend to and families to feed. If a militia member was not inclined to serve the time required when his regiment was mustered, he had three options: he could not report for the muster; he could desert; or he could find an American officer, offer his parole, and be excused from taking part in the war.

It was relatively easy for a colonist to ignore the call to muster and pay any fines levied against him for not reporting. In 1812 the largest fine that could be imposed for not attending a muster was £20, and given that in peacetime the average annual income of a farmer with thirty to forty acres of land was at least £110, not reporting made financial sense, especially when inflation due to the war doubled the cost of food. Job Lodor from London District stated that when the general call for the militia was sounded, he would simply "go home & secure his many goods & property" and wait for his fine.[10]

When the colonists deserted from their posts, they were not deserting to the enemy but were deserting back to their farms or businesses. The men would turn out if they thought they were needed for a battle, but the idea of sitting and waiting on garrison duty or working on roads did not sit well with them. After all, many of the musters were called during the most critical times for farming, and a farmer spending a prolonged period away from his farm would not be able to provide for his family.[11] Commanding officers, when faced with widespread desertions, simply dismissed the militia and sent the remaining men home rather than use the regular military to round up the deserters to face punishment. This prevented any serious repercussions against the colonist, did not waste badly needed regular troops on policing duties, and allowed the officers to save face and give the appearance that they were in control of what was happening in the field.[12]

When York was overrun by American forces at the end of July 1813, many Upper Canadians discovered a new way to avoid militia duty. The captured Upper Canadian militia members were given their freedom in exchange for their parole, or forswearing any further military duty for the remainder of the conflict. Traditionally, parole was offered only to prisoners captured during a battle. However, clever colonists such as Michael Corts, who lived a day's journey from York, travelled with his sons to York in search of the American parole tribunal to offer their parole and seek an exemption from military duty, even though they were nowhere near York the day of the battle. As rumours spread, many Upper Canada residents believed that all eligible males in any district where an American victory occurred automatically acquired paroles. This led to thousands of Upper Canadians who believed they were exempt from militia duty.[13]

Not all colonists attempted to get out of militia duty. According to John Strachan in an 1814 letter to the prince regent, 50 percent of eligible colonists served willingly in the militia in 1812 and at least one-third served in 1813.[14] One such willing militia member was Daniel Yake, a Pennsylvania German who left Strausberg, Germany, in 1785 with his wife and children. His wife died on the voyage to America, and he eventually married Mary Nicely in Pennsylvania. The family, which included Esther, Daniel, Hiram, Gabriel, John, and Jacob, came with their parents to Upper Canada about 1804 and settled in York County in the Stouffville-Altona area. When war was declared, Daniel was among the farmers willing to serve in the militia, despite his age, for by then he was over seventy years of age!

The militia mustered and trained in several locations, including the Vanderburg/Robert Marsh property near Yonge Street in Richmond Hill, and were honoured by a visit from General Brock before they were given a three-week leave to return home and plant their crops. Unlike his father, one of Daniel Yake's sons refused to serve in the militia, as he feared he might have to fight his old friends and neighbours from Pennsylvania. As a result, he was imprisoned in the York Gaol during the war.

While Daniel was serving in the Niagara area and at the Battle of Lundy's Lane in 1814, he sent several bags of flour across Lake Ontario to York for his family to ensure that they had an adequate supply for cooking and baking. When he was discharged and returned home, he found that the flour had not reached his family and they had survived on wild game and pumpkins from their root cellar. Daniel walked from the Stouffville Sideroad to the wharf at York in search of the flour and eventually found one bag that he carried home on his back — a total journey of sixty miles![15]

Another willing militia man was Henry Lapp, originally from Hamburg, Germany. Henry came to Canada after he was "bought off" from army service in his native land. When he arrived in Canada, he immediately joined the militia and participated in the defence of York. It is said that he fired the last shot before the Americans captured the town. After the war, he settled near Cedar Grove in Markham.[16]

In addition to their roles in the battles on Upper Canada's soil, the militia was often required to provide a defence of their homes and property. American raiding parties, sometimes led by Upper Canadian renegades such as Joseph Willcocks, targeted Upper Canadian farms and businesses for looting and destruction. This wanton destruction of private property and direct threat to their families and livelihoods enraged the local colonists and spurred them to action, forgetting their misgivings about the war in the defence of their homes and families.

On November 11, 1813, Colonel Henry Bostwick and a small force of Dover militiamen ambushed and killed five American raiders and captured another sixteen at Nanticoke Creek. They were hailed as heroes and were mentioned in the general orders issued to other residents: "Observe how quickly the energetic conduct of 45 individuals has succeeded in freeing the inhabitants of an extensive district from a numerous and well-armed banditti who would have left them neither liberty nor prosperity."[17] Colonists in the Niagara region responded similarly to American raiding, prompting Major Daniel MacFarland of the U.S. Army to write to his wife that "the whole population is against us ... not a foraging party but is fired on, and not infrequently returns with missing members."[18]

In the western part of the province, with little action from the American invaders, few members of the militia ever faced the enemy in battle, but they still provided a significant contribution to the war effort:

The militia's most significant contribution to the war effort was not on the battlefield and does not appear in official dispatches. The militia made up a great part of the different garrisons, so allowing the regular troops to act in the field. They also formed the bulk of the men who maintained the commissariat, constructed the roads, and laboured at the king's works. They built fortifications and blockhouses, cleared land around the fortified posts, and aided the building of the Royal Navy's ships that sailed on the Great Lakes.

Without doubt, a key to the success of the British in repulsing the American invasion of this country was the support and to a marked degree the mere quiescence of the Native inhabitants in the west. Their goodwill was ensured and cemented by the provision to them of vast quantities of trade goods and foodstuffs transported from Montreal. Detachments of militia were regularly called upon to move these convoys of bateaux up the St. Lawrence and, after the control of the Lakes was lost in early 1813, overland by road and water to the northwest.[19]

These duties allowed the regular military to do what they had the training and equipment to do — fight the enemy!

The Upper Canadians were not interested in fighting a war with the United States. Many of them still had families, friends, and business partners south of the border. When war was declared, they often sought to avoid the conflict because it interfered with their primary concern: making a living and ensuring the survival of their families. However, when American forces threatened their families and livelihoods, the militiamen responded with strength and helped push the invaders from their country.

16

....

DEEDS SPEAK

"THE BANNER is beautiful!" exclaimed the young women seated around it, busily embroidering the Crown Royal of England in crimson and gold, with the wreath of laurel leaves in shades of green just below it, as they kept admiring their work. It had been designed many months ago by their friend and fellow needlewoman, twenty-one-year-old Mary Warren Baldwin, and they had began work on it immediately. How generous of Mrs. McGill to have invited them to work on it in her home and how fortunate they were with the stream of gentlemen visitors who came by with words of encouragement, including the handsome, vigorous, powerfully built man of action, forty-three-year-old Isaac Brock, who was engaged to one of their number, Miss Sophia Shaw. Donald McLean and the law student, John Beverley Robinson, who read aloud "The Battle of Talavera" and other stirring poems of hard-fought battles and great victories won, had also visited them.[1]

The new rector, John Strachan, newly arrived in York from Kingston, had chosen the motto for the banner: DEEDS SPEAK. He hoped the new little church, St. James, would be completely finished in time for the dedication and presentation of the banner to the 3rd Regiment of York Militia as a token of their pride and grateful thanks to that company of charming, handsome, and brave young men!

Little did they know as they sat chatting and later gossiping over their teacups in the parlour what lay in store for the soldiers they admired so much and the banner they had worked on with such zeal.

When the banner was finished, it was presented at an evening service at St. James' Church in York late in 1812 and was attended by "the 3rd Regiment and all the respectable inhabitants of the town." By then the stunning British victory at Detroit in August had seen the men of the 3rd Regiment of York Militia flank companies, led by Major William Allan, participate, spurring the young ladies to complete the banner. By this time, too, Brock had been tragically killed at the Battle of Queenston Heights in October. His last words were rumoured to have been to Major Allan and the 3rd Regiment: "Push on the brave York Volunteers." However, this is unlikely, since Brock was nowhere near the York Volunteers and was surrounded by his old regiment, the 49th, during the battle.[2] Everyone attending the evening service had also known young Lieutenant-Colonel John Macdonell, a York lawyer and aide-de-camp to Brock who had led another charge and was also killed.[3]

Reverend John Strachan blessed the regimental colours and the standard to be presented, while Anne Powell, daughter of the Honourable Mr. Justice Powell, spoke:

The young ladies of York, in presenting a banner to you, their brave and successful defenders, perform a duty most grateful to their own feelings.

They are proud to imitate the example of the most distinguished of their sex; among the most virtuous and heroic nations who have rejoiced in giving public testimony of their gratitude to their countrymen — returning from victory — receive then this ensign of union as a token of their lasting esteem and the harbinger of increasing glory.

Receive it as a proof that they strongly participate in that generous patriotism which burns with so pure a flame through the Province, and when you behold it unfurled on the day of battle, let it become a kind remembrancer of the unlimited confidence which they place in the efficiency of your protection.[4]

Finally, Major William Allan addressed his regiment:

Gentlemen of the 3rd Regiment of York Militia, — Permit me to express the great satisfaction I feel in meeting you upon this occasion. The inestimable gift conferred upon you by the young ladies of York must awaken the most lively gratitude in every bosom, and suggest new motives for redoubled efforts for resisting the enemy. They rely in our conduct and courage, not merely in defending the banner which they have presented, but in making it the admonisher of the most important services in support of our King and country; and you are not to suppose that this religious dedication of your colors is an unmeaning ceremony, for they become a token and pledge of a most solemn engagement, not only between us and our sovereign, who calls us to arms, but between us and our fellow-subjects, for whose protection we are employed, especially of that tender and most amiable sex who have consigned them to our hands, and who zealously hope that we will never abandon them but with life.

It is our part to realize these grateful expectations, and to show that they have not been consecrated by words only, but by our hearts, and by the noble and heroic spirit which the sight of them shall always awaken in our hearts.

The enemy against whom we contend are loud in their threats, and enraged at the unexpected resistance which they have already experienced in this province; they will wreak the bitterest vengeance upon us should they prove victorious, but they can never be victorious while we are united: on the contrary, they will continue daily to receive bloody proofs that a country is never more secure than when defended by its faithful, loyal and industrious inhabitants, who have constantly before their eyes the tenderest pledges of nature, and are influenced by all that is dearest and most interesting to the human heart.[5]

On April 27, 1813, an American force attacked and destroyed York. Many accounts of that fateful day survive. However, one of the coincidences was that the chiefs and warriors of the Mississauga Nation were holding a Grand Council on their land west of York on the morning of April 27 as enemy troops boarded small boats and rowed ashore, landing nearby. The First Nations rallied in the nearby woods in defence of the town and were soon joined by a company of regular troops but were badly outnumbered and only managed to delay the enemy advance on the fort.[6] One of the most interesting and lively eyewitness accounts of the two explosions that shook Fort York — first a battery magazine and then the grand magazine — was given by P. Firnan, the young son of one of the soldiers in the Royal Newfoundland Regiment engaged in the fort's defence

While this part of our forces was contending with the enemy in the woods, an unfortunate accident happened in the battery opposite to the fleet which proved a death blow to the little hope that might have been entertained of a successful issue to the proceedings of the day. A gun was aimed at one of the vessels, and the officers, desirous of seeing if the ball would take effect, ascended the bastion. In the meantime the artilleryman, waiting for the word of command to fire, held the match behind him as is usual under such circumstances and the travelling magazine, a large wooden chest containing cartridges for the great guns, being open just at his back, he unfortunately put the match into it, and the consequence, as may be supposed, was dreadful indeed. Every man in the battery was blown into the air. The officers were blown from the bastion by the shock, but escaped with a few bruises; the cannons were dismounted, and consequently the battery was rendered completely useless.

I was standing at the gate of the garrison when the poor soldiers who escaped the explosion, with a little life remaining, were brought into the hospital, and a more affecting sight could scarcely be witnessed. In consequence of the loss of the battery and the reduction that had been made in the number of our troops, their ground was no longer tenable, but after nobly and desperately withstanding their enemies for several hours a retreat towards the garrison became inevitable, though every inch of the ground was obstinately disputed.

The government house, with some smaller buildings, formed a square at the centre battery, and under it the great magazine, containing a large quantity of powder, was situated. As there were only two or three guns at this battery, and it but a short distance from the garrison, the troops did not remain in it, but retreated to the rear. When the Americans, commanded by General Pike, reached this small battery, instead of pressing forward, they halted, and the General sat down on one of the guns; a fatal proceeding, for in a few minutes his advance guard, consisting of about three hundred men and himself, were blown into the air by the explosion of the grand magazine.

Some time before this horrible circumstance took place the vessels had commenced firing on the garrison, which obliged the females and children leaving it. We therefore retired into the country to the house of an officer of the militia, but feeling anxious to know the fate of the day I left the house without the knowledge of my mother and was proceeding towards the garrison when the explosion took place. I heard the report, and felt a tremendous motion in the earth, resembling the shock of an earthquake, and, looking towards the spot, I saw an immense cloud ascend into the air.

At first it was a great confused mass of smoke, timber, men, earth, etc., but as it broke it assumed the shape of a vast balloon. When the whole mass had ascended to a considerable height, and the force by which the timbers, etc., was impelled upwards became spent, the latter fell from the clouds as it spread over the surrounding place.

I then advanced towards the garrison. I discovered our little party between the town and that place which latter they had not proceeded much further when [they] had been obliged to evacuate.[7]

It is from the *Diary* of Ely Playter that we learn more of the events of that fateful day. When Playter realized the seriousness of the situation in the town and at the garrison, he had the presence of mind to "advise Mrs. Chapman a Woman that Cooked for us [at the fort] to come away."[8] Mrs. Chapman escaped unharmed, for when Playter returned three days later he related: "I got some of my things Mrs. Chapman had saved for me in Garrison."[9]

Meanwhile the women who had worked on the banner and their children had taken refuge in the McGill house located on rising ground and sheltered by the forest behind, which was considered less vulnerable than the houses near the bay. Suddenly, Donald McLean "burst into the drawing-room with the banner the ladies had worked wrapped about his body for concealment, and remembered the storm raised by Miss Powell's bitter words of indignation and her taunt that after all their protestations the men had sent the banner back for the women to protect."[10]

They buried the banner under a tree in the orchard behind the house, first wrapping it in an old bit of canvas. When the Americans evacuated York, the banner was rescued, restored to the regiment, and carried through every engagement in which the 3rd York took part.

SECOND LETTER FROM MARTHA

Big Creek Bridge
Now Heron's Bridge
Yonge Street
Upper Canada
December 30, 1812

Dear Sister Mary,

Our worst fears came to pass over the past summer when President Madison of the republic to the south of us declared war and tried to invade us so we would be another of his states. It happened in June, and we heard about it by the end of the month from travellers on our road, but our newspaper in York did not print a notice of if until weeks later on July 11. My mistress always wants the paper, as do I, as she, too, is a reader and we can barter for it with any kind of produce at Mr. Tiers's store in York.

The enemy troops crossed over our border in July and again in October and again last month, trying to make us surrender, but our brave soldiers and our militia men and our Native warriors have beaten them back. Some of the young men I have walked out with are in the militia and had to go long distances to fight at the village near Amherstburg and at the village of Queenston where our best general and his aide were both killed. There is a story, often repeated, of Maria Hill, a soldier's wife who, during the battle, was brave enough to boil her pots and kettles of water to make tea and to cut slabs of bread to feed our hungry men who had not eaten all day. She carried out her baby and hid him in the shelter of a woodpile so he could watch. What a brave woman Maria was to do that! I pray that I will never be tested by this war for I fear that I would fail.

There has been some good news from the far north as we took one of their forts by surprise — it is the one with a long name, Michilimackinac. There is much talk in the inn about it. Our crops were good this year, and we had oats and hay in abundance and were able to sell some to the army last month in York. They advertised for beef, but we had none to spare. We have much more traffic on this road now and must be wary of running low in supplies. My mistress keeps an eagle eye on all. She is a wonderful Frenchwoman.

Another day and we will have the new year upon us. We pray that peace will not be far behind.

With love,
Your sister Martha

17

· ·

FORTUNE ASSISTS THE BRAVE[1]

THERE ARE many unexpected acts of bravery in everyday life, and the outcome is always uncertain. Fortune, chance, timing, luck all play a part in the success or failure of a person or enterprise. This was particularly true during the eventful years between the end of the American Revolution and the conclusion of the War of 1812. Let us consider just two acts of unexpected bravery by two people. In simple terms they both "took a walk" over well-known terrain a few miles distant and a few days apart.

On June 12, 1796, Elizabeth Simcoe told of her visit to the home of Adam Green and his family:

> Green's wife died a year ago and left ten children, who live here with their father in a house consisting of a room, a closet and a loft; but being New Jersey people, their house is delicately clean and neat, and not the appearance

of being inhabited by three people, every part is so neatly kept.[2]

Adam Green held over six thousand acres of land in New Jersey when the American Revolution began, but like thousands of other Loyalists he was forced to flee with his family. When they arrived in Upper Canada, they were granted three hundred acres near the hamlet of Stoney Creek. It was there on February 4, 1796, that Adam's wife, Martha, gave birth to Billy, believed to be the first white child born in the area. Sadly, she passed away soon after.

Raised by his older sisters, Billy loved the outdoors and grew to know the surrounding forests, plants, animals, birdcalls, paths, trails, tracks, and hiding places by heart. When the war started, teenage Billy and his three older brothers joined the 5th Regiment of the Lincoln Militia and often drummed for militia musters while their older brother, Levi, played the fife.[3]

On a sunny Sunday morning, June 5, 1813, Billy and Levi were out scouting along the ridge near their homes. Levi and his wife, Christine (Tina), and their two-year-old daughter, Hannah, lived nearby on a five-acre farm and operated a mill. The two young men were transfixed as they watched in horror as an enormous American army marched by on the track below. Unknown to them, their brother-in-law, Isaac Corman, husband to their sister, Keziah (Desire, Dezia, Kezi), had just been arrested for being rude to an American officer and had been taken to the fire-damaged King's Head Inn where American regiments were awaiting supplies. When the Americans learned that Isaac was from Kentucky, he was released and was given the password to travel through the American lines and return home.

En route Isaac met Billy, who persuaded him to share the password.[4] Billy headed straight for British headquarters on Burlington Heights to share this crucial information and describe the American army that had arrived and camped on the Gage farm near Stoney Creek.

Meanwhile a British officer at the Heights, Lieutenant James FitzGibbon, had volunteered to masquerade as a farm girl selling butter and visit the American camp to find out all he could about their plans. He was successful, and with this additional information the British attacked in the darkness.

The following morning as dawn broke the Gage farm fields revealed the chaos and horror of the unexpected nighttime attack by the British. The Americans retreated to Fort George, leaving wagons, baggage, tents, and dozens of dead and wounded behind. Crude hospitals were set up in the Gage farmhouse, the nearby Nash and Davis homes, and Dr. Case's house near Hamilton, with British surgeons tending to the wounded from both armies.

Billy, along with three other lads from Stoney Creek, Peter Gage, John Lee, and John Yaeger, used William Gage's stoneboat and yoke of oxen to bury the U.S. dead on the knoll behind the battlefield.[5]

As the remnants of the American army retreated to Fort George, the British pursued them and set up a command post and supply depot in the farmhouse of John DeCew at Beaver Dams, with James FitzGibbon in charge.

Meanwhile, in the village of Queenston, Laura Ingersoll Secord was coping with her daily round of nursing, housekeeping, and survival under very difficult circumstances. Laura was the thirty-seven-year-old daughter of a Massachusetts Loyalist and wife of James Secord, a prosperous merchant who had served in the militia and was badly wounded at the Battle of Queenston Heights. The mother of five children, Laura never knew when Americans might knock on her door and demand food, drink, and lodging. One of her granddaughters, Laura Secord Clark, believed that, while a group of American soldiers were eating a meal in her home, Laura overheard their plan to take the DeCew post and James FitzGibbon, whom they despised. Laura realized that the British must be warned and left home at 4:30 a.m. on the morning of June 22. The events that were set in motion are described in detail on her monument in Drummond Hill Cemetery, Lundy's Lane, Niagara Falls:

To Perpetuate
The Name and Fame of
LAURA SECORD
who walked alone nearly 20 miles by a circuitous, difficult and perilous route through woods and swamps and over miry roads to warn a British outpost at DeCew's Falls of an intended attack and thereby enabled Lieut.

> FitzGibbon on the 24 June 1813, with less than 50 men of H.M. 49th Regt., about 15 militia men, and a small force of Six Nations and other Indians under Captains William Johnson Kerr and Dominique Ducharme, to surprise and attack the enemy at Beechwoods (or Beaver Dams) and after a short engagement to capture Col. Boerstler of the U.S. Army and his entire force of 542 men with two field pieces.[6]

These two acts of bravery, like hundred of others during this period, were recognized and remembered by friends, neighbours and colleagues, but it took some time for them to be officially recognized as something more than local legend and folklore.

When the Prince of Wales, later King Edward VII, visited Canada in 1860, he heard of Laura and her incredible exploit. He requested a meeting with her and was so moved by her story when he visited her home that he gave her a gift of £100. For the teenage Billy Green it was October 1875, when he was a senior citizen, that he was recognized and honoured as a surviving veteran of the War of 1812. The Dominion government showed its gratitude with an award of $20 a year in recognition of his indispensable services in this famous battle.[7] Two monuments, one on the battlefield near Battlefield House, National Historic Site, and the other in the nearby cemetery, pay tribute to the first native son in Stoney Creek.

18

....

"For They Hanker After Rebellion"[1]

Joseph Willcocks, the youngest son of a country gentleman, was born in 1773 a few miles from
Dublin. Joseph was well educated, handsome, and
determined to follow his kinsman, William Willcocks,
to Upper Canada. He set sail in December 1798, and
after seventy-four days of stormy seas, reached New
York City on February 12 of the following year. By
stagecoach and sleigh, he arrived in York in March,
joined his kinsman, and stayed at William's home for a
time while he searched for a position.

The Honourable Peter Russell, a first cousin of
William Willcocks, appointed Joseph his private secretary in his office as receiver general on May 1. Joseph
continued to sleep and breakfast with William but spent
the rest of his time at the Russells's. He petitioned for a
lot in York and received an acre near the centre of the
small town in a few days. Willcocks and Russell recommended him for twelve hundred acres, which he
received in the Township of Hope in June 1801.

Later in 1801 "he had left his kinsman's entirely and became one of Russell's family, from which change he derived 'many essential advantages, one in particular by associating with the first Person in the Country and another by having all the comforts that this world could possibly afford.'"[2] This must have pleased Joseph, as he appears to have been a social climber, watching for every opportunity to advance himself and his position in society.

During this period, Joseph kept a diary of social visits, pleasure parties, meals, and menus, giving us an insight into everyday life in the new capital:

19th. [September, 1800] I went to the Humber on a pleasure party with Mr. & Miss Russell, Mr. and the Miss Willcocks's Mr. Weeks and Doctor Baldwin We left York at 10 oClock and reach'd the Humber in Mr. Jarvis's Boat at half past 12. Walked about for an hour & dined at half past 1 We had for Dinner a piece of Cold Roast Beef, Cold ham cold chickens & hot stewed Wild Ducks. We all arrived safe at home at 5 oClock in the Evening.

28th. Dined at Mr. Willcocks it being Sunday Mr. Gamble dined there We had for dinner a piece of roast Beef and a Pudding Returned home to Tea Dennison & his son George spent the Evening with us Mr. Russell and Doctor Baldwin were striving to fix a Microscope but could not do it complete. Mr. Russell read part of Gullivers Travels. The whole of the day there was very fine Weather Bought six salmon for Mr. Russell for a Dollar.

30th. I dined with Mr. Small Rugless [James Ruggles, merchant and magistrate] was there We had for dinner a Salmon two Perch a piece of Roast Beef a Brace of Pheasant rashers and Peas I spent the Evening at home Willcocks was there Mr. Russell read part of Gullivers Travels ...

3rd. [October, 1800] ... Went a shooting to the Island — got nothing — Returned to Dinner and had a Loin of roast Mutten, a Broiled Chicken and Some Pork a Bread Pudding Went to Willcocks's after Dinner & from thence to a Puppet Shew the Performance was very indifferent, the Weather very fine.

Thursday [December] 25. [1800] Went to Church Weekes dined with us we had for dinner soup roast beef boiled Pork Turkey Plumb Pudding & minced pies We had a supper for the first time in my remembrance I came to bed at 12 It was a very fine day Playter called for some camomile.

Thursday. January 1. [1801] Miss Russell & I went out in the sled We called at Alcocks,

McGills McCawleys & Smiths I upset the sled coming home McGill the two Ridouts the Solicitor Gen'l & Ruggles called to pay their respects We had for dinner Boiled beef, a roast Pig & minced meats. Denison called in the evening. It froze the bay across I went to bed at 10.

Saturday, 28. [March, 1801] ... We tapped a Cask of Madaira — we had for dinner minced veal soup Pigs cheek Eggs & Pudding Mr. Ridout & Mr. Denison called in the evening. I went to bed at 8 oClock. Mr. Willcocks gave a large supper party ...

Friday, 3. [April, 1801] ... Went to church, a vessell arrived from Kingston the first this year I met Mr. Givens and Mrs. Peters Mrs. Peters & I went to Mr. Jarvis's then to Mr. Alcock's where we met Mrs. Jarvis & Mrs. McGill we came home with Mrs. Jarvis & then went to every store in the town I returned to dinner and had roast veal trout Soup Ducks Pancakes ...

Monday, 27. Went before breakfast to the farm staid there until night Returned and saw some Indians fighting I parted them One of them attempted to Strike me I nocked him down they were then quiet Dined when I came home on roast fowl & Pudding. Mr. Willcocks called we play cards.

Monday, 8. [June, 1801] Wrote in the office for some time I went to Dr. Gamble to buy a Yoke of Oxen but he was too Dear I brought an acct. from the office to the Parliament House I had for Dinner corned beef cold veal fish & Pudding. The whole Town was Illuminated for the victories obtained by the English.

Thursday, 2. [July, 1801] I went to the Election for a Member for the Home County Mr. Small & Mr. McDonell were candidates Mr. Baldwin came here we voted for Small I Examined McDonnell's Voters Returned to dinner and had Salmon Roast veal & Pudding Mr. Baldwin slept with us.

Sunday, 19. Went to Church with Mrs. Smith Returned home with Mr. & Mrs. McCawley called at McGills returned home to Dinner ... Drank Tea at Mr. McGills on my [way] there I called at Mr. Weekes's & after some conversation he said that I was under the Pay of Government as their Informer & used many other approbious imputations — I gave him the Lye he said I should fight him to Morrow. I agreed to fight but not so soon —

Monday, 20. Captn. De Hean called on me in the morning to know my time and place — I told him 6 Next Morning at the point of the Don — I then went to Mr. Ruggles to get him to be my second he agreed he lay with me that night — the Hour was changed from 6 to 5.

Tuesday, 21 At 4 oClock Ruggles and I were going to the Place appointed when the Sheriff met us & Put us under an arrest — I gave security before Mr. Jarvis to keep the peace for Six Months.[3]

Despite having been challenged to a duel and having to give security to keep the peace for six months, all appeared to be going well for Joseph until August 1802 when Peter Russell terminated "his delightful and profitable association" because of Joseph "presuming to court his sister Elizabeth [actually his half-sister], an unpardonable offence."[4]

Russell and Chief Justice Allcock were not on good terms, and Allcock invited Joseph to a meeting. Soon Joseph was happily placed as marshal of Assize, registrar of the Court of Probate, and sheriff of the Home District, and living in Allcock's home.

He had got over his desire to marry Miss Russell, but if he remained unmarried it was because he could not bring himself "to form a lasting connection to any of the Ladies of this Country, they have an air of inconsistency about them that Europeans cannot very well brook with."[5]

Joseph began to take a greater interest in the legislature about this time, and would have known its history and followed it closely as changes were made:

Colonel John Graves Simcoe was appointed Lieutenant Governor of Upper Canada, 1791: he met his Executive Council at Kingston, in July 1792; and July 16, 1792, he issued a Proclamation dividing the Province into nineteen counties and fifteen constituencies, one constituency, Kent, to send two representatives.

The constituency containing Toronto was composed of Durham, York and the First Riding of Lincoln, stretching from the western boundary of Northumberland, the present "Town-line" just east of Port Hope, to the "grand river to be called the Ouse" (now the Grand River), down this river to the "Indian Road leading to the Forks of the Chippewa Creek (which creek is now to be called the Welland)," then down this creek, &c. The constituency stretched from Lake Ontario back to the tract "belonging to the Messisague Indians."[6]

By 1805, friends and colleagues noticed a great change in Joseph. He was no longer catering to those in power but was "particular friends" with William Weekes and Robert Thorpe, well-known malcontents. Thorpe was elected to represent "the Counties of Durham and Simcoe and the East Riding of the County of York" in his friend's place, for Weekes had been killed by a brother lawyer in a duel in October 1806 at the American Fort Niagara.[7] A few months later Thorpe announced the publication at Niagara of the *Upper Canada Guardian or Freeman's Journal,* a very controversial newspaper, with Joseph Willcocks as editor.

The following year Joseph took the oath "representing the West Riding of the County of York, the First Riding of the County of Lincoln, and the County of Haldimand, came within the Bar and took his seat accordingly."[8] Months of tumult ensued in Parliament as Joseph fluctuated between loyal member and troublemaker. In 1807 he was dismissed as sheriff for joining the opposition.[9]

When the House met, February 3, 1812, war was in the air: Isaac Brock, the President, who had replaced Gore, recognized the danger — he recognized, too, the existence of a very considerable disloyal element of Republican proclivities anxious that Upper Canada should became part of the United States. In the Speech from the Throne he urged the necessity of the "adoption of such measures as will best secure the internal peace of the Country and defeat every hostile aggression." The House resolved that it would "use every exertion in its power to enable His Honor to put the

Province in a state to defend themselves against every hostile aggression"; and Willcocks moved, seconded by Benajah Mallory (who afterwards shared his treason) for a Select Committee to draft an address to Brock. The Address, unanimously adopted, spoke of the astonishment of the House at the conduct of the United States and their "infatuated partiality" to France, their "insulting threats," &c., and assured His Honor that the House would "pay early attention to the adoption of such measures as shall appear to us best calculated to secure the internal peace of the Country and defeat every hostile aggression."[10]

Joseph joined Brock's forces as a volunteer, served valiantly at Queenston Heights, and was mentioned with commendation in the General Orders of October 21, 1812, that contained the official account of the battle. However, Joseph was soon showing a different side of his character. By 1813 he appears to have decided the invaders would be victorious and formed a corps of traitors and renegades called the Canadian Volunteers, who rode about the Niagara Peninsula helping the Americans. Abraham Markle and Benajah Mallory, both gentlemen and former members of the Upper Canada House of Assembly, joined his band in plundering, destroying property, and harming their former neighbours and friends. His Canadian Volunteers were involved in some of the greatest outrages of the war, including the burning of Newark on December 10, 1813:

The inhabitants were given twelve hours notice to remove themselves and their property, and then Willcocks, a former resident, and his men put Newark to the torch. An American officer remembered the renegade leader leading "a banditti through the town ... setting fire to his neighbours dwelling" and "applying the epithet of Tory to all who disapproved of this flagrant act of barbarity." By morning, the pretty little community of eighty structures, one of the oldest settlements in Upper Canada, was reduced to smoking ruins.[11]

Joseph was wearing an American colonel's uniform when he was killed on September 5, 1814, by a Canadian or British marksman while he was commanding a unit of the Canadian Volunteers and setting a guard at Fort Erie after it had been taken by American troops.[12]

So ended the life and checkered career of a young man who had found acceptance among the social and political leaders of Upper Canada and who had fought valiantly for his new homeland before turning to lawlessness, disloyalty, treachery, and the most notorious acts of cruelty to his former neighbours, friends, and colleagues.

19

"LORD, HAVE MERCY ON MY POOR COUNTRY"[1]

AS THE war continued and escalated in late 1813, the level of anxiety and fear grew among those "at home" tending their families, farms, and shops. When local militiamen returned to their farms to plant or harvest their crops, or to prepare for the next battle, apprehension was fuelled by the stories they told. In addition, U.S. Major-General Jacob Brown, commander of the New York frontier, sent out countless scouting and raiding parties, hoping to gain information and throw the defenders off balance. These parties were often guided by the turncoat Joseph Willcocks and his infamous Canadian Volunteers, who knew the local areas. The residents feared and hated those patrols and fought back, for as William Merritt described them, "plundering every house they could get at: they even plundered women of everything they had."[2]

Everyone was constantly on the alert for news or unexpected occurrences. The arrival of British regulars and their Native allies in the area was a clear signal that trouble was about to erupt and homes, barns, crops, live-stock, and lives were at risk, for the enemy must be nearby. Not only was there an approaching battle, but the tales of armies appropriating homes, barns, and outbuildings for their headquarters and hospitals were legendary. That was exactly what happened on an autumn day on a farm near the Thames River and Moraviantown.

On the afternoon of October 5, 1813, David Sherman and his friend Ward were looking for the family's cows when they spied some unusual activity in the nearby black ash swamp. David was the fifteen-year-old son of Lemuel Sherman, a member of the Kent Militia. When they investigated, the lads found Tecumseh, known as the Great Shawnee Chief, sitting on a newly felled tree, with a scarf wound around his head and a large white ostrich plume stuck in it. Surrounding him were about three hundred Native warriors. Tecumseh advised the boys to round up the cows and get them into the barn as quickly as possible, since they were expecting an American attack. Attack they did, and it was there that Tecumseh lost his life.

The following morning Lemuel and David Sherman helped other local farmers to bury the dead from both armies in a common grave.[3] Local legends claimed they had witnessed Tecumseh's burial and knew its location. However, extensive research by archaeologists and historians is documented in detail in Guy St-Denis's book *Tecumseh's Bones* without a firm solution or conclusion to the mystery.[4]

The sick and wounded were left on the Sherman farm, and the family's barn was used as a hospital where many men spent the winter recovering and carving their names in the boards and beams of the building. One of the Kentucky troops remained behind and made his home with the Sherman family until his death many years later when he, too, was buried on the farm.[5]

In early October U.S. Major-General James Wilkinson decided to take Montreal. When he proceeded down the St. Lawrence River with a large fleet of boats carrying over seven thousand troops, he was astonished that the Canadian militia hurried to the riverbank where they hid behind trees and rocks, shooting at the invaders at every opportunity. Colonel Joseph Morrison with about seven hundred men and thirty warriors from the Mohawk Nation were in hot pursuit, and the battle was joined on the farm fields of Captain John Crysler of the Dundas Militia. Wilkinson and Major-General Morgan Lewis, to whom he had delegated his authority, both lay ill in boats on the river while the battle raged on November 11.

With the defeat of the American forces, it was left to Crysler, his neighbours, and their sons to bury the dead from both armies, tidy up the battlefields, and rebuild the split-rail fences. Crysler's fields of fall wheat had been totally destroyed. Dr. William "Tiger" Dunlop, who was stationed at Fort Wellington, was assigned the challenging task of caring for the wounded. He was billeted in the upper room of the home of a Dutch family that had fled to Upper Canada after backing the Crown during the American Revolution. Dunlop enjoyed the immaculate and well-furnished home and the meals that included "a profusion of meat, fish, eggs, cakes and preserves." He made sure, however, that he was always away tending his wounded on Saturday mornings, since it was the grand cleaning day for the family.[6]

A few miles down the river shore, Loyalist Michael Cook and his family were trying to recover from the ravages of having their log tavern commandeered by the invading U.S. forces as their headquarters and then being bombarded by the defending British soldiers. Mrs. Cook and the children had hidden in the cellar until the battle had ended and then emerged to discover that the retreating Americans had looted and carried away a strange assortment of necessities, including one hundred bushels of wheat, twenty-five sheep, eighteen white blankets, three silk shawls, ten calico gowns, one set of calico bed curtains, one string of gold beads, and half a bushel of salted sausage![7]

December 1813 brought one of the most appalling events of the war and was described briefly in the previous chapter. The Loyalist militia officer William Hamilton Merritt saw a glare in the sky at Twelve Mile Creek on the night of December 10. He realized that the whole of the Town of Niagara was ablaze and rode hard to be confronted by a terrible sight:

Nothing but heaps of coal and the streets full of furniture that the inhabitants had been fortunate enough to get out of their homes met the eye in all directions. Mr. Gordon's house, my old quarters, was the only one left standing. The garrison was abandoned. Many tents left standing, the barracks and woodworks nearly consumed ... Little could be saved and the burning extended to homes along the River Road towards Queenston.[8]

Merritt was incensed by the destruction, and like all the British forces when they learned of the devastation, was determined to get revenge for the innocent victims.

Third Letter from Martha

Heron's Bridge
Yonge Street
Upper Canada
December 31, 1813

Dearest Mary,

What a terrible year it has been for us all in Upper Canada. The enemy has crossed over time and time again to raid our farms and villages of food and animals, and to burn mills, homes, and barns, leaving many families in sore straits. They came by Lake Ontario to York and took the town and the fort, and people fled in all directions. One of York's ladies, Elizabeth Russell, loaded her phaeton with her most precious belongings, and with her servant driving she walked with four friends and their children to Baron Frederick de Hoven's log house on his farm in the village of Eglinton on the west side of Yonge Street between here and York. That house is only two rooms — one above the other. So with nine more visitors they must have been very crowded! After a few days, some of the ladies walked home again. One of the children was so young that his mother had to carry him in her arms all the way there and home again.

A young lad named Firnan arrived in York to visit his father who was with a Newfoundland regiment and saw the terrible sights of the fort exploding and York being burned by the Americans. Firnan has described it to many travellers who have told us all about that day while they stayed with us here at the inn.

Not long after the enemy again crossed and took Fort George, making our men move inland. One brave boy helped our troops. His name was Billy Green, who smuggled the enemy password to our troops.

We have lost many battles on the lakes, and it is hard to move any food now. The enemy has destroyed so many mills and farms with their crops in the fields and carried off everything they could that we are often left with empty larders.

Oh, dear Mary, I do not think we can win this war, after all, and what shall I do if we lose? I do not know if the school will open again and I do not have the coin for the passage home, and I know that I could not bear to live here. Pray for me, dear Mary, and indeed for us all.

Your sister,
Martha

20

WHEN THINGS ARE AT
THEIR WORST THEY
BEGIN TO MEND[1]

WITH THE continued raids and assaults by the Americans in 1814 and the loss of farmland, crops, and livestock, food supplies became crucial for the military and civilians. It was soon learned that the distilling of grain into whisky and the export of most farm produce was banned. Other measures were soon taken by Lieutenant-General Drummond at Kingston: "I therefore have been under the necessity of ordering all the women and children, of the Troops, to be sent down from Niagara, Burlington and York [to Lower Canada], and families of the Indians to be placed on Half Allowance, with a view to decreasing as much as possible the issues."[2]

Young Thomas Ridout, former student of John Strachan, was by then the deputy assistant commissary general and described the strange business of finding food for the troops as he moved to Cornwall:

There are 1,600 troops there to be fed, and my duty will be hard, for the country is so excessively poor that our supplies are all drawn from the American side of the river. They drive droves of cattle from the interior under pretence of supplying the army at Salmon River, and are allowed to pass the guards, and at night cross them over to our side. I shall also be under the necessity of getting most of my flour from their side.[3]

The Americans did not give up despite their defeat in Crysler's fields, for by July 1814 the farm of Samuel Street on the Niagara River near Chippawa became a bloody battleground. Samuel, a native of Connecticut, came to the area during the American Revolution to sell supplies to the British army and stayed to marry his sweetheart, Sarah, have a family, and develop a prosperous farm. Merchant, land speculator, judge, member of the provincial legislature, and paymaster of the militia were among his credentials.

Pine Grove Farm was a well-ordered property with fields of oats and peas enclosed with split-rail fences, tons of hay in the barn, and a wharf on the river. There were two houses on the farm, Samuel's own and a second where his daughter, Mary, and her husband, John Ussher, lived. When Mary realized the horror about to be unleashed on that hot July day, she drove the family's large herd of dairy and beef cattle to safety on the north side of the Chippawa River, leaving behind two dairy cows with their calves, fifteen shoats (young pigs), and a riding mare. Needless to say, the Americans took those animals when they retreated.[4]

The Street buildings sat on a large, open, flat area often described as a plain, surrounded by a pine woods, and it became the site of the short but bloody Battle of Chippawa on July 5, 1814. The farmhouse became a hospital where the medical personnel worked tirelessly to treat the wounded. Conditions were just as bad in the village of Chippawa, for Captain Hamilton Merritt arrived with his troop of militia shortly after the battle ended and found that "every house was filled with the wounded."[5]

Before the end of July the two forces met again when the Americans attacked, this time in the lane and farm fields of William Lundy, a Quaker and Loyalist who had settled in 1786 about a mile from Niagara Falls. The battle began on July 25, stretched into the darkness of the night, and was described the following morning by an American doctor:

> The dead had not been removed during the night, and such a scene of carnage I never beheld, particularly at Lundy's Lane, red coats and blue and grey were promiscuously intermingled, in many places three deep, and around the hill ... the carcasses of 60 and 70 horses disfigured the scene.[6]

It was at this battle that Dr. Dunlop struggled to carry wounded men on his back to the temporary hospital, thus saving many lives. It was here, too, that William Merritt was taken prisoner, and when the Americans burned the bridge at Chippawa, threw their heavy baggage into the rapids above Niagara Falls, and withdrew to Fort Erie, he was taken along.[7]

James FitzGibbon, the Irish daredevil often called "The Green Tiger" and the milkmaid in disguise at Stoney Creek, survived the Battle of Lundy's Lane untouched and decided that this was the time to undertake another daring mission. He had long been in love with Mary Haley, daughter of George Haley, a former British soldier who had served in the American Revolution and had later received a land grant near Adolphustown in what became Leeds County.

Mary had endeared herself to James when she heard the stories of soldiers going barefoot on the Niagara frontier. She knew she could not make him shoes, but she could knit him enough socks to last in the coming campaigns ... if he never stopped marching!

James requested and received permission from his colonel for a three-day leave and rode horseback for the two-hundred-mile journey. Meanwhile Mary and Reverend George Okill Stuart travelled thirty miles from Kingston to Adolphustown to meet him. Their marriage certificate, filed in the Synod Office of St. George's Cathedral in Kingston, confirms that "James FitzGibbon, Captain in his Majesty's Glengarry Lt. Infantry Fencibles, was married to Mary Haley (by licence) by me George Okill Stuart on the 14th day of August, 1814."[8] James then said goodbye to his bride on the church steps and rode back to his regiment to keep his word to his commanding officer.

In 1814, Joseph Carroll, an expert saddler and harness maker, was ordered by the military authorities to remove from Niagara to York. Joseph and his wife and family of eight sons were accustomed to "being on the move" and the adventures that resulted. Carroll had come to the colonies with his Irish parents and had served with the British artillery during the American Revolution. He settled in New Brunswick on a small, poor lot of land where he met and courted his wife. Later he journeyed to Upper Canada, met Brock, and was promised a thousand-acre grant of land for his service in the army. The family left New Brunswick in 1809 and travelled by water to New York and eventually by springless lumber wagon and ferry to Queenstown.[9] They lived at Ten Mile Creek for the next two years but were unable to procure the promised land grant because the Land Department deferred its location "till matters became more settled." The family then moved to the Grand River country where they resided at Fairchild's Creek on a farm owned by Mohawk chief Thomas Davis.[10]

Joseph joined the army in 1813 as a volunteer "master collar maker," since he was too old for enlistment. His two oldest sons, James and William, were enlisted as drivers and harness makers.[11] Mrs. Carroll and the four younger children survived in uncertain accommodation in the Niagara area until Joseph was taken prisoner at Fort Niagara and later paroled. Despite being given his parole, Joseph returned to military service and was posted to York, since "it would be death for him if he had fallen into enemy hands" and he "could attend to such duty in his department as lay farthest from the lines."[12]

John Carroll, one of Joseph's young twin sons, shared his memories of the journey and safe haven for the family in York in 1814:

> The government had provided for our transport in something like a schooner, called the *St. Vincent*, named after General Vincent. She was a poor old craft ... very frail ... there were several military men on board ... who were being sent from the dangers of the "lines" to the hospitals at the capital ... About the third night we entered Toronto Bay and moored under the guns of the "New Garrison" ... Soldiers' families were not allowed in the barracks, but a friendly artillery man, Mr. Elder, shared his hut with mother and children.[13]

This family had now existed over the war years in an unfurnished house, a hole in the ground, a loft over a military blacksmith shop, and finally in a hut! York became their abode until the close of the war.

Despite the steady stream of news describing the skirmishes, shortages, and doom and gloom, the tide had actually turned in the conflict and the American dream that the republic could be expanded was fading fast. Families like the Carrolls and newlyweds such as James and Mary would soon be making plans for the future. Peace talks were already underway in Belgium, and on Christmas Eve 1814, Britain and the United States signed the Treaty of Ghent.

FOURTH LETTER FROM MARTHA

Heron's Bridge
Yonge Street
Upper Canada
January 13, 1815

My dear sister Mary,

Happy New Year! My prayer is that every day of this new year will be filled with happiness for you and our family. Our happiness here in Upper Canada depends on whether the whispers and rumours of peace are true. Ever since Christmas Eve the story has been on everyone's lips and we wait to hear the outcome. Alas, we do not know if life will ever be the same again after this terrible time. We have tried to keep the doors of the inn open for travellers and some food for their needs, but we have been sore oppressed as the military has needed so many supplies and spirits to keep them going.

The farmers hereabouts are called to military duty many times, their poor families have to tend the animals and fields, and many crops are lost so they cannot pay their credit at the stores. For the men who have been killed or wounded and families left fatherless or plundered, there is a helpful group called the Loyal and Patriotic Society. It was started by the inhabitants of York who gave private subscriptions and the labour of the young ladies there when all realized that the militia had neither arms nor warm clothing to take up their duties between Niagara and Fort Erie. Subscriptions have come from Quebec and Montreal, from our sister colony of Nova Scotia, from the island of Jamaica, and of course from dear England, too, as his Royal Highness the Duke of Kent is the patron of the group. Examples include £15/12 shillings 10 pence given to Mrs. Kendrick, the widow of Lieutenant Duke William Kendrick, who had the Potashery on Yonge Street in York and was killed on duty in the Garrison of York, and another £17/15 shillings given to Andrew Borland, who served at Detroit, Queenston, and York where he was severely wounded. There are so many more, and the society has done its best to ease their suffering.

If the war is indeed finished, I will close my book of scraps and memories and put it away in a safe place to read when I am older. Do you remember that saying we learned in school from the Greek historian Herodotus — in peace sons bury their fathers and in war fathers bury their sons? It is true and it is happening here and must stop!

Oh, I pray the rumours are true and that we can now live in peace.

With my love, your sister
Martha

AFTERWORD

....

THE PEACE OF CHRISTMAS EVE 1814

THE TREATY of Ghent was concluded on December 24, 1814, with an agreement to return to the *status quo ante bellum* — pre-war conditions. The news did not travel very swiftly, and as a result skirmishes and battles continued in the early weeks and months of 1815. Despite the call for the pre-war status quo, many communities were changed forever by the invading armies that raided, stole, and destroyed homes, property, crops, and livestock.

Perhaps the greatest change was in the attitudes of Canadians to their neighbours, communities, and country. They had been invaded with the assumption that they would willingly become another state in the union of the republic, but they had found common cause with a unique set of partners — British troops, local militia, fur traders, farmers, and First Nations — to repel the invaders and protect their property and future.

There was an economic period of depression as prices dropped when the commissariats slowed or stopped purchasing food and supplies from farmers and merchants. Attention was turned to repairing and rebuilding the communities that had been devastated and the forts and posts that had been destroyed.

There was hope in the land and in the hearts of the people as the *York Gazette* reported on April 15, 1815: "The [Lake] Ontario uncommonly high — The ice disappeared from the bay of York a fortnight earlier than in the two preceding seasons — Immense flights of the wild pigeon — from west to east — The wild ducks revisit our waters since peace was made."

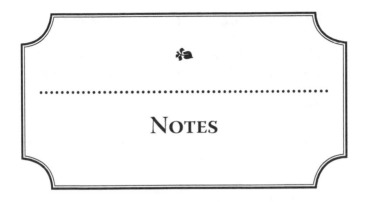

NOTES

Introduction: Setting the Stage

1. Wesley B. Turner, *The War of 1812: The War That Both Sides Won*, 2nd ed. (Toronto: Dundurn Press, 2000), 17.
2. Andrew F. Hunter, *The History of Simcoe County* (Barrie, ON: Simcoe County Historical Society, 1909) 21–22. James became a distinguished lawyer and later a chief justice of Lower Canada. William Cowan was the grandson of a well-known fur trader near Matchedash Bay, but with both parents dead, he was being raised by his maternal grandmother.

Chapter 1: From the Beginning of Time

1. I.L. Martinello, *Call Us Canadians* (Toronto: McGraw-Hill Ryerson, 1976), 175.
2. Carl Benn, *The Iroquois in the War of 1812* (Toronto: University of Toronto Press, 1998), 26.
3. Mary Alice Downie and Mary Hamilton, *'and some brought flowers': Plants in a New World* (Toronto: University of Toronto Press, 1980), *passim*.
4. Richard Merritt, Nancy Butler, and Michael Power, eds., *The*

Capital Years: Niagara-on-the-Lake 1792–1796 (Toronto: Dundurn Press, 1991), 224–25.

5. Helen Caister Robinson, *Mistress Molly, the Brown Lady: A Portrait of Molly Brant* (Toronto: Dundurn Press, 1980), 7.
6. *Ibid.*, 158; and Mary Beacock Fryer, *Bold, Brave, and Born to Lead: Major General Isaac Brock and the Canadas* (Toronto: Dundurn Press, 2004), 142.
7. J. Ross Robertson, ed., *The Diary of Mrs. John Graves Simcoe* (Toronto: William Briggs, 1911), 119.

Chapter 2: "Thank God, We Are No Longer in Dread"

1. William H. Tippet, "The Hannah Ingraham Story," United Empire Loyalists' Association, *Annual Transactions* (1904–13): 116.
2. *Ibid.*, 117–18.
3. James Richardson, "Notes on Early Settlements," The Women's Canadian Historical Society of Toronto, *Annual Report and Transaction* 15 (1915–16): 30. Michael Grass had been taken prisoner by the French during the Seven Years' War and was held at Frontenac (present-day Kingston).
4. *Ibid.*, 30–32.
5. Mrs. Burritt, "The Settlement of the County of Grenville," The Ontario Historical Society, *Papers and Records* 3 (1901): 106.
6. Elizabeth Hicks, *A True Romance of the American War of Independence 1775–1783* (London: William Hardwick, Peckham, 1903), 9.
7. *Ibid.*, 15.
8. *Ibid.*, 32–33.
9. *Ibid.*, 38–53. There are no dates given in Elizabeth's accounts, but this would appear to be the winter of 1777–78 or the spring of 1778.

10. *Ibid.*, 85–86.
11. *Ibid.*, epilogue, page 2.

Chapter 3: "The Amount of Flesh or Fish Required"

1. W.S. Wallace, "Fort William of the Fur Trade," *The Beaver* (December 1949): 16; and *Fort William: Hinge of a Nation*, feasibility study prepared by National Heritage Limited for the Province of Ontario (author's collection), 36.
2. Alexander Henry, *Travels and Adventures in Canada and the Indian Territories Between the Years 1760 and 1776* (New York: I. Riley, 1809), *passim*.
3. Dorothy Duncan, *Canadians at Table: Food, Fellowship, and Folklore, a Culinary History of Canada* (Toronto: Dundurn Press, 2006), 47.
4. Grace Lee Nute, *The Voyageur's Highway* (St. Paul, MN: Minnesota Historical Society, 1951), 54.
5. Elliott Coues, ed., *New Light on the Early History of the Greater Northwest*, vol. 1 (New York: F.P. Harper, 1897), *passim*.
6. *Ibid.*, 20.
7. Gabriel Franchère, *Narrative of a Voyage to the Northwest Coast of America*, 2nd ed. (Chicago: Redfield, 1854), 335.
8. Donald McPherson, *Fur Trade Journal, Lac La Pluie* (November 13, 1817).
9. Daniel Harman, *A Journal of Voyages and Travels in the Interior of North America* (Toronto: George N. Morang, 1904), 111.
10. John McKay, *River Lake La Pluie Journal 1793–1794 and 1794–1795*, Hudson's Bay Archives, Microfilm B.105/a/5.
11. V.A. MacDonald, "Major-General Sir Isaac Brock," The Ontario Historical Society, *Papers and Records* 10 (1913): 7.

Chapter 4: "The Apprehension of War"

1. Mary Beacock Fryer, *Elizabeth Posthuma Simcoe 1762–1850: A Biography* (Toronto: Dundurn Press, 1989), 32.
2. *Ibid.*, 35.
3. Mary Quayle Innis, ed., *Mrs. Simcoe's Diary* (Toronto: Macmillan of Canada, 1965), 44.
4. *Ibid.*, 45–46.
5. *Ibid.*, 123.
6. *Ibid.*, 64.
7. *Ibid.*, 88–89.
8. J. Ross Robertson, ed., *The Diary of Mrs. John Graves Simcoe* (Toronto: William Briggs, 1911), 244.
9. *Ibid.*, 156.
10. *Ibid.*, 328.
11. Innis, *passim.*
12. *Ibid., passim.*

Chapter 5: "In the Shelter of the Fort"

1. Alan Gowans, *Building Canada: An Architectural History of Canadian Life* (Toronto: Oxford University Press, 1966), 10. The full quotation is: "In the shelter of the fort, the evolution from wilderness to settled community is completed."
2. Leslie F. Hannon, *Forts of Canada: The Conflicts, Sieges and Battles That Forged a Great Nation* (Toronto: McClelland & Stewart, 1969), 164.
3. *Ibid.*, 164.
4. François Alexandre Frederic, Duc de la Rochefoucauld-Liancourt, "Travels Through the United States of America, the Country of the Iroquois, and Upper Canada, in the Years 1795, 1796, and 1797," in *Kingston! Oh, Kingston! An Anthology*, Arthur Britton Smith, ed. (Kingston, ON: Brown & Martin, 1987), 86–87.
5. Hannon, 262.

6. Dennis and Carol Farmer, *The King's Bread, 2nd Rising: Cooking at Niagara 1726–1815* (Youngstown, NY: Old Fort Niagara Association Inc., 1989), 15.

7. *Ibid.*, 12.

8. *Ibid.*, 15.

9. Richard Merritt, Nancy Butler, and Michael Power, eds., *The Capital Years: Niagara-on-the-Lake 1792–1796* (Toronto: Dundurn Press, 1991), 96.

10. *Ibid.*, 31.

11. Library and Archives Canada, NMC 153/2 Fort Erie.

12. George Seibel, *The Portage Road: 200 Years 1790–1990* (Niagara Falls, ON: City of Niagara Falls, 1990), 215.

13. Mary Quayle Innis, ed., *Mrs. Simcoe's Diary* (Toronto: Macmillan of Canada, 1965), 76.

14. J. Long, *Voyages and Travels of an Indian Interpreter and Trader* (London, 1791), 16.

15. Edwin, C. Guillet, *Pioneer Settlements* (Toronto: Ontario Publishing Company, 1933), 139–42.

16. *Ibid.*, 145.

17. Accessed at *www.parkhousemuseum.com*.

18. *The Duff-Bâby Mansion* (Les Amis Duff-Bâby, 2010), brochure.

19. Frederick Armstrong, *Toronto: The Place of Meeting* (Toronto: Windsor Publications, 1983), 20–22.

20. *Great Britain, Treaties, Indian Treaties and Surrenders* (Ottawa, 1891), 1.34.

21. Innis, 95.

22. Bruce West, "Dublin or Don," *Globe and Mail*, October 18, 1968, 25.

23. Armstrong, 31.

24. J.N. Emerson, H.E. Devereux, and M.J. Ashworth, *A Study of Fort St. Joseph* (Ottawa: National Historic Parks and Sites Branch, Parks Canada, Department of Indian and Northern Affairs, 1977), 143.

25. Hannon, 261.

Chapter 6: "When the Journey's over There'll Be Time Enough to Sleep"

1. A.E. Housman, from "Reveille," in *A Shropshire Lad* (Mineola, NY: Dover Publications, 1990), 4.
2. Mary Quayle Innis, ed., *Mrs. Simcoe's Diary* (Toronto: Macmillan of Canada, 1971), 71.
3. *Ibid.*, 163.
4. *Ibid.*, 163.
5. J. Ross Robertson, ed., *The Diary of Mrs. John Graves Simcoe* (Toronto: William Briggs, 1911), 320.
6. *Ibid.*, 323.
7. Edwin C. Guillet, *Pioneer Settlement in Upper Canada* (Toronto: University of Toronto Press, 1969), 64.
8. *Ibid.*, 65–66.
9. Margaret McBurney and Mary Byers, *Tavern in the Town: Early Inns and Taverns in Ontario* (Toronto: University of Toronto Press, 1987), 66.

Chapter 7: "Peace Be to This House, and to All That Dwell in It"

1. *The Book of Common Prayer* (Oxford, Eng.: Clarendon Press, 1827), 199.
2. Mary Beacock Fryer, *Elizabeth Posthuma Simcoe 1762–1850: A Biography* (Toronto: Dundurn Press, 1989), 51–52.
3. A.H. Young, "Letters from the Secretary of Upper Canada and Mrs. Jarvis to Her Father, the Reverend Samuel Peters, DD," The Women's Canadian Historical Society of Toronto, *Annual Report and Transaction* 23 (1922–23): 32–33.
4. Catherine F. Lefroy, ed., "Recollections of Mary Warren Breckenridge," The Women's Canadian Historical Society of Toronto, *Transaction* 3 (n.d.): 1–2.
5. *Ibid.*, 3.

6. Edith Firth, *The Town of York 1793–1815* (Toronto: University of Toronto Press, 1962), 234, 270.

7. Gerald M. Craig, ed., *Early Travellers in the Canadas* (Toronto: Macmillan of Canada, 1955), 7.

Chapter 8: "We Plough the Fields, and Scatter the Good Seed on the Land"

1. "We Plough the Fields, and Scatter" by Jane Montgomery Campbell, accessed at *www.bartleby.com/294/536.html*.

2. *Life on the Farm* (Toronto: Ontario Ministry of Agriculture and Food, 1984), 2.

3. *Ibid.*, 3.

4. *Ibid.*, 3; and Richard Merritt, Nancy Butler, and Michael Power, eds., *The Capital Years: Niagara-on-the-Lake 1792–1796* (Toronto: Dundurn Press, 1991), 17.

5. L.H. Tasker, "The United Empire Loyalist Settlement at Long Point, Lake Erie," The Ontario Historical Society, *Papers and Records* 2 (1900): 54–55.

6. Loris Russell, *Everyday Life in Colonial Canada* (Toronto: Copp Clark, 1973), 26–27.

7. Metropolitan Toronto Library, Baldwin Room, *Elizabeth Russell Papers*, February 24, 1794.

8. G.G. Marquis, ed., *Great Canadians* (Toronto, 1903), 183.

9. Mary Quayle Innis, ed., *Mrs Simcoe's Diary* (Toronto: Macmillan of Canada, 1965), 112.

10. Patricia Hart, *Pioneering in North York* (Toronto: General Publishing, 1968), 11.

11. Loris Russell, "First Farms and the Development of Agriculture," in *Everyday Life in Nineteenth Century Ontario* (Toronto: Ontario Museum Association, 1978), 17.

12. *Fort William: Hinge of a Nation* (Toronto: National Heritage, 1970), 16.

Chapter 9: When One Door Shuts Another Opens

1. The chapter title is derived from a sixteenth-century proverb.
2. "The Colony of French Émigrés in York County, Ontario — 1798," The Women's Canadian Historical Society of Toronto, *Annual Report and Transaction* 25 (1924–25): 11, 14, 16, 17.
3. *Ibid.*, 20.
4. *Upper Canada Gazette*, January 27, 1803.
5. *Ibid.*, December 17, 1803.
6. *Ibid.*, February 20, 1808.
7. Patricia Hart, *Pioneering in North York: A History of the Borough* (Toronto: General Publishing, 1968), 213, 215.
8. G.E. Reaman, *The Trail of the Black Walnut* (Toronto: McClelland & Stewart, 1957), 147.
9. *Upper Canada Gazette*, January 3, 1802.
10. Hart, 194.
11. *York Gazette*, August 29, 1812.
12. *Kingston Gazette*, November 13, 1813.
13. Dorothy Duncan, "What Jane Austen Would Have Seen in York in 1802," Ontario Genealogical Society, *Families* 45, no. 2 (2006): 82–83.
14. *Ibid.*, 82–83.
15. Edith Firth, *Town of York, 1793–1815* (Toronto: The Champlain Society, 1962), 128.
16. *Ibid.*, lxxxv.

Chapter 10: Desperate Diseases Must Have Desperate Remedies

1. The chapter title is derived from a sixteenth-century proverb.
2. Matilda Coxe Stevenson, "Ethnobotany of the Zuñi Indians," *Thirtieth Annual Report of the American Bureau*

of Ethnology to the Secretary of the Smithsonian Institution, 1908–1909 (Washington, DC: Government Printing Office, 1915), 39.

3. Margaret Conrad, Alvin Finkel, and Cornelius Jaenen, *History of the Canadian Peoples*, vol. 1 (Toronto: Copp Clark Pitman, 1993), 93.

4. Mary Alice Downie and Mary Hamilton, *'and some brought flowers': Plants in a New World* (Toronto: University of Toronto Press, 1980), 75.

5. *Ibid.*, 16.

6. *Ibid.*, 143.

7. *Ibid., passim.*

8. Craig Heron, *BOOZE: A Distilled History* (Toronto: Between the Lines, 2003), 31.

9. Library and Archives Canada, RG 19E5(a) (War of 1812 Losses Claims), 3741: file 3.

10. *Simcoe County Pioneer Papers* (Barrie, ON: Simcoe County Historical Society, 1908), Chapter 3, 15.

11. Gilbert Collins, *Guidebook to the Historic Sites of the War of 1812* (Toronto: Dundurn Press, 2006), 264.

12. Richard Merritt, Nancy Butler, and Michael Power, eds., *The Capital Years: Niagara-on-the-Lake 1792–1796* (Toronto: Dundurn Press, 1991), 231.

13. Mary Quayle Innis, ed., *Mrs Simcoe's Diary* (Toronto: Macmillan of Canada, 1971), 184.

14. *Biography of Mrs. Lydia B. Bacon* (Boston: Massachusetts Sabbath School Society, 1856), 25–26.

15. Hannah Jarvis, *H. Jarvis Cookbook, and Health Remedies*, circa 1811.

Chapter 11: Knowledge Is Power

1. The chapter title is derived from a sixteenth-century proverb.

2. Patricia Hart, *Pioneering in North York* (Don Mills, ON: General Publishing, 1968), 95.

3. *Historical Glimpses of Lennox and Addington* (Lennox and Addington County Council, 1964), 144.

4. Edith Firth, *The Town of York 1793–1815* (Toronto: University of Toronto Press, 1962), 89.

5. *Ibid.*, lxxiv.

6. Hart, 95.

7. Matilda Edgar, *Ten Years in Upper Canada* (Toronto: William Briggs, 1890), 26.

8. *Ibid.*, *passim*.

9. Edwin C. Guillet, *Pioneer Settlements* (Toronto: Ontario Publishing Company, 1933), 17.

10. Firth, 209.

11. Leo A. Johnson, *History of the County of Ontario 1615–1875* (Corporation of the County of Ontario, 1973), 62.

12. M. Audrey Graham, *150 Years at St. John's York Mills* (Toronto: General Publishing, 1966), 20.

13. W.H. Higgins, *The Life and Times of Joseph Gould* (Toronto: C.B. Blackett Robinson, 1887), 39.

Chapter 12: "Strange to See How a Good Dinner and Feasting Reconciles Everybody"

1. The chapter title is derived from a 1665 entry in Samuel Pepys's *Diaries*.

2. Frances L. Whisler, *Indian Cookin'* (Nowega Press, 1973), 31.

3. Frances McNaught and Margaret Taylor, *The Early Canadian Galt Cook Book* (Toronto: William Briggs, 1898), 380.

4. Dorothy Duncan, *A Valuable Book of Receipts* (Toronto: Ontario Museum Association, 1981), 7.

5. Hannah Jarvis, *H. Jarvis Cookbook, and Health Remedies*, circa 1811, 9.

6. Margaret MacDonald, *Whistler's Mother's Cook Book* (New York: G.P. Putnam's Sons, 1979), 115.
7. *Biography of Mrs. Lydia B. Bacon* (Boston: Massachusetts Sabbath School Society, 1856), 42.
8. MacDonald, 99.
9. James Macfarlane, *The Cook Not Mad or Rational Cookery* (Kingston, Upper Canada, 1831), 37.
10. Dennis and Carol Farmer, *The King's Bread 2nd Rising* (Youngstown, NY: Old Fort Niagara Association Inc., 1989), 60.
11. *Ibid.*, 61.
12. Versions of this simple recipe appeared in many hand-written and printed cookery books in the nineteenth and early twentieth centuries, including *The Dominion Cook Book* by Ann Clarke, published in 1899, as pudding continued to be a staple item at our ancestors' tables.
13. Jarvis, 4–5.

Chapter 13: The First Blow Is Half the Battle!

1. Oliver Goldsmith, *She Stoops to Conquer* (Mineola, NY: Dover Publications, 1991), act 2, scene 1.
2. J.N. Emerson, H.E. Devereux, and M.J. Ashworth, *A Study of Fort St. Joseph* (Ottawa: National Historic Parks and Sites Branch, Parks Canada, 1977), 25.
3. George Thomas Landmann, *Adventures and Recollections of Colonel Landmann*, vol. 1 (London: Colburn and Co., 1852), 327.
4. John Abbott, Graeme S. Mount, and Michael J. Mulloy, *The History of Fort St. Joseph* (Toronto: Dundurn Press, 2000), 74, 77.
5. David Lee, *The Fort on St. Joseph's Island* (Ottawa: National Historic Parks and Sites Branch, Parks Canada, Manuscript Report Series, No. 131, 1966), 9.

6. Gilbert Collins, *Guidebook to the Historic Sites of the War of 1812* (Toronto: Dundurn Press, 2006), 257.

Chapter 14: "I Have a Large Bag on the Pommel of My Saddle"

1. *Biography of Mrs. Lydia B. Bacon* (Boston: Massachusetts Sabbath School Society, 1856), 42. The quotations in this chapter are taken from an edited version of the hand-written record of Lydia Bacon's experiences in 1811–12, which was published in 1856, three years after her death. In the early 1830s, Lydia herself created a manuscript from letters she wrote to her family and entries from her journal, placing everything in chronological order. This unedited text was published in two parts and can be found in: Mary M. Crawford, ed., "Mrs. Lydia B. Bacon's Journal, 1811–12," parts 1 and 2, *Indiana Magazine of History* 40, no. 4 (1944): 367–86; 41, no. 1 (1945): 59–79.
2. *Ibid.*, 20.
3. *Ibid.*, 25.
4. *Ibid.*, 27.
5. *Ibid.*, 34.
6. *Ibid.*, 30.
7. *Ibid.*, 32.
8. *Ibid.*, 39–40.
9. *Ibid.*, 40–41.
10. *Ibid.*, 42–44.
11. *Ibid.*, 45–48.
12. *Ibid.*, 54–55.
13. *Ibid.*, 56–57.
14. *Ibid.*, 59–60.
15. Wesley B. Turner, *The War of 1812: The War That Both Sides Won* (Toronto: Dundurn Press, 2000), 42–43.
16. *Biography of Mrs. Lydia B. Bacon*, 64–65.

17. *Ibid.*, 66.
18. *Ibid.*, 67–69.
19. *Ibid.*, 69–70, 72, 74–77.
20. *Ibid.*, 85.

Chapter 15: "A Well-Regulated Militia Is of the Utmost Importance"

1. From the 1808 Amendment to the Militia Act of 1793. A fuller quotation is: "Whereas a well-regulated militia is of the utmost importance to the defence of this Province ..."
2. Pierre Berton, *The Invasion of Canada 1812–1813* (Toronto: McClelland & Stewart, 1980), 142.
3. Wesley B. Turner, *The War of 1812: The War That Both Sides Won* (Toronto: Dundurn Press, 2000), 27.
4. William Gray, *Soldiers of the King: The Upper Canadian Militia 1812–1815* (Erin, ON: Boston Mills Press, 1995), 26.
5. *Ibid.*, 26.
6. *Ibid.*, 26.
7. Berton, 142.
8. George Sheppard, *Plunder, Profit, and Paroles: A Social History of the War of 1812 in Upper Canada* (Montreal and Kingston: McGill-Queen's University Press, 1994), 41–42.
9. Michael Smith, *A Geographical View of the Province of Upper Canada and Promiscuous Remarks on the Government*, 2nd ed. (Trenton, ON: Moore & Lake, 1813), 80–81.
10. Sheppard, 61.
11. Gray, 34.
12. Sheppard, 65.
13. *Ibid.*, 87–88.
14. G.W. Spragge, *The John Strachan Letterbook: 1812–1834* (Toronto: The Ontario Historical Society, 1946), 30.
15. Isabel Champion, *Markham 1793–1900* (Markham, ON:

Markham Historical Society), 105, 165, 290. Additional information found in the City of Pickering Archives by Lorne Smith, historian for the Town of Markham.

16. William R. Wood, *Past Years in Pickering: Sketches of the History of the Community* (Toronto: William Briggs, 1911), 257.

17. Sheppard, 93–94.

18. *Documentary History of the Campaign on the Niagara Frontier*, 9 volumes, E.A. Cruikshank, ed. (Welland, ON: Lundy's Lane Historical Society, 1902–08), 1:73.

19. Gray, 43–44.

Chapter 16: Deeds Speak

1. Mary Beacock Fryer, *Bold, Brave, and Born to Lead: Major General Isaac Brock and the Canadas* (Toronto: Dundurn Press, 2004), 7.

2. Pierre Berton, *The Invasion of Canada, 1812–1813* (Toronto: McClelland & Stewart, 1980), 253.

3. Edith Firth, *The Town of York 1793–1815* (Toronto: University of Toronto Press, 1962), 191.

4. Mary Agnes FitzGibbon, "A Historic Banner: A Paper Read on February 8th, 1896," The Women's Canadian Historical Society of Toronto, *Transaction* 1 (n.d.): 15–16.

5. *Ibid.*, 17.

6. *The City and the Asylum* (Toronto: Museum of Mental Health Services, 1993), 13.

7. Matilda Edgar, "The Explosion of the Magazine at York, Now Toronto, 27th April 1813," The Women's Canadian Historical Society of Toronto, *Transaction* 8 (1914): 7–8.

8. Firth, 280.

9. *Ibid.*, 282.

10. FitzGibbon, 20.

Chapter 17: Fortune Assists the Brave

1. The title of the chapter is taken from a fourteenth-century proverb.
2. J. Ross Robertson, ed., *The Diary of Mrs. John Graves Simcoe* (Toronto: William Briggs, 1911), 328.
3. James Elliott, *Billy Green and the Battle of Stoney Creek, June 6, 1813* (Stoney Creek, ON: Stoney Creek Historical Society, n.d.), 5–6.
4. The password was the first three syllables of General William Henry Harrison's name "Will-Hen-Har." See Mabel Thompson, "Billy Green the Scout," The Ontario Historical Society, *Ontario History* 4 (1952): 179.
5. *Ibid.*, 177.
6. Enid L. Mallory, *The Green Tiger: James FitzGibbon, a Hero of the War of 1812* (Toronto: McClelland & Stewart, 1976), 61–62.
7. Thompson, 181.

Chapter 18: "For They Hanker After Rebellion"

1. The chapter title is derived from King William I of England's purported deathbed speech in 1087 when he said: "For they hanker after rebellion, cherish sedition, and are ready for any treachery."
2. William Renwick Riddell, "Joseph Willcocks, Sheriff, Member of Parliament, and Traitor," The Ontario Historical Society, *Ontario History* 24 (1927): 477.
3. Edith Firth, *The Town of York 1793–1815* (Toronto: University of Toronto Press, 1962), 232–35.
4. Riddell, "Joseph Willcocks, Sheriff," 478.
5. *Ibid.*, 479.
6. William Renwick Riddell, "Toronto in the Parliaments of Upper Canada, 1792–1841," The Women's Canadian Historical Society of Toronto, *Transaction* 22 (1921–22): 13.

7.   Riddell, "Joseph Willcocks, Sheriff," 479–80.
8.   *Ibid.*, 481.
9.   Ernest A. Cruikshank, "A Study of Disaffection in Upper Canada in 1812–15," in *The Defended Border*, Morris Zaslow, ed. (Toronto: Macmillan of Canada, 1964), 217.
10. Riddell, "Joseph Willcocks, Sheriff," 486.
11. Donald E. Graves, *Red Coats & Grey Jackets: The Battle of Chippawa, 5 July 1814* (Toronto: Dundurn Press, 1994), 7.
12. Riddell, "Joseph Willcocks, Sheriff," 488.

Chapter 19: "Lord, Have Mercy on My Poor Country"

1.   The chapter title is derived from the purported last words of Scottish politician Andrew Fletcher in 1716 when he supposedly said in reference to Scotland: "Lord, have mercy on my poor country that is so barbarously oppressed."
2.   Wesley B. Turner, *The War of 1812: The War That Both Sides Won* (Toronto: Dundurn Press, 2000), 94.
3.   Katherine B. Coutts, "Thamesville and the Battle of the Thames," The Ontario Historical Society, *Papers and Records* 9 (1910): 22, 24.
4.   Guy St-Denis, *Tecumseh's Bones* (Montreal and Kingston: McGill-Queen's University Press, 2005), 142.
5.   Coutts, 24.
6.   William Dunlop, *Tiger Dunlop's Upper Canada* (Toronto: McClelland & Stewart, 1967), 17.
7.   Margaret McBurney and Mary Byers, *Tavern in the Town* (Toronto: University of Toronto Press, 1987), 14.
8.   Jack Williams, *Merritt: A Canadian Before His Time* (St. Catharines, ON: Stonehouse Publications, 1985), 19.

Chapter 20: When Things Are at Their Worst They Begin to Mend

1. The chapter title is derived from a sixteenth-century proverb.
2. William Weeks, "The War of 1812: Civil Authority and Martial Law in Upper Canada," in *The Defended Border*, Morris Zaslow, ed. (Toronto: Macmillan of Canada, 1964), 202–03.
3. Thomas G. Ridout to Thomas Ridout, January 19, 1814, in *Ten Years in Upper Canada*, Matilda Edgar, ed. (Toronto: William Briggs, 1890), 269.
4. Donald E. Graves, *Red Coats & Grey Jackets: The Battle of Chippawa, 5 July 1814* (Toronto: Dundurn Press, 1990), 79–80.
5. Jack Williams, *Merritt: A Canadian Before His Time* (St. Catharines, ON: Stonehouse Publications, 1985), 20.
6. Alan Taylor, *The Civil War of 1812* (New York: Alfred A. Knopf, 2010), 395.
7. Williams, 22.
8. Enid L. Mallory, *The Green Tiger: James FitzGibbon, a Hero of the War of 1812* (Toronto: McClelland & Stewart, 1976), 109–10.
9. John Carroll, *My Boy Life* (Toronto: William Briggs, 1882), 6, 9.
10. *Ibid.*, 34, 42.
11. *Ibid.*, 50.
12. *Ibid.*, 62.
13. *Ibid.*, 72, 75.

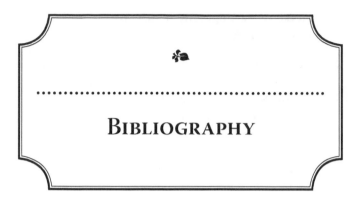

BIBLIOGRAPHY

Abbott, John, Graeme S. Mount, and Michael J. Mulloy. *The History of Fort St. Joseph*. Toronto: Dundurn Press, 2000.

Armstrong, Frederick. *Toronto: The Place of Meeting*. Toronto: Windsor Publications, 1983.

Benn, Carl. *The Iroquois in the War of 1812*. Toronto: University of Toronto Press, 1998.

Berton, Pierre. *The Invasion of Canada 1812–1813*. Toronto: McClelland & Stewart, 1980.

Biography of Mrs. Lydia B. Bacon. Boston: Massachusetts Sabbath School Society, 1856.

Burritt, Mrs. "The Settlement of the County of Grenville." The Ontario Historical Society, *Papers and Records* 3 (1901).

Carroll, John. *My Boy Life*. Toronto: William Briggs, 1882.

Champion, Isabel. *Markham 1793–1900*. Markham, ON: Markham Historical Society, 1979.

The City and the Asylum. Toronto: The Museum of Mental Health Services, 1993.

Collins, Gilbert. *Guidebook to the Historic Sites of the War of 1812*. Toronto: Dundurn Press, 2006.

"The Colony of French Émigrés in York County, Ontario — 1798." The Women's Canadian Historical Society of Toronto, *Annual Report and Transaction* 25 (1924–25).

Conrad, Margaret, Alvin Finkel, and Cornelius Jaenen. *History of the Canadian Peoples*, vol. 1. Toronto: Copp Clark Pitman, 1993.

Coues, Elliott, ed. *New Light on the Early History of the Greater Northwest*, vol. 1. New York: F.P. Harper, 1897.

Coutts, Katherine B. "Thamesville and the Battle of the Thames." The Ontario Historical Society, *Papers and Records* 9 (1910).

Craig, Gerald M., ed. *Early Travellers in the Canadas, 1791–1867*. Toronto: Macmillan Company of Canada, 1955.

Cruikshank, E.A. "A Study of Disaffection in Upper Canada in 1812–15," in *The Defended Border*, edited by Morris Zaslow. Toronto: Macmillan Company of Canada, 1964.

Cruikshank, E.A., ed. *Documentary History of the Campaign on the Niagara Frontier*, 9 volumes. Welland, ON: Lundy's Lane Historical Society, 1902–08.

Downie, Mary Alice, and Mary Hamilton. *'and some brought flowers': Plants in a New World*. Toronto: University of Toronto Press, 1980.

Duc de la Rochefoucauld-Liancourt, François Alexandre Frederic. "Travels Through the United States of America, the Country of the Iroquois, and Upper Canada in the Years 1795, 1796, and 1797," in *Kingston! Oh, Kingston! An Anthology*, edited by Arthur Britton Smith. Kingston, ON: Brown & Martin, 1987.

The Duff-Bâby Mansion. Les Amis Duff- Bâby, 2010, brochure.

Duncan, Dorothy. *Canadians at Table: Food, Fellowship, and Folklore, a Culinary History of Canada*. Toronto: Dundurn Press, 2006.

_____. *A Valuable Book of Receipts*. Toronto: Ontario Museum Association, 1981.

_____. "What Jane Austen Would Have Seen in York in 1802." Ontario Genealogical Society, *Families* 45 (2006), no. 2.

Dunlop, William. *Tiger Dunlop's Upper Canada*. Toronto: McClelland & Stewart, 1967.

Edgar, Matilda. "The Explosion of the Magazine at York, Now Toronto, 27th April 1813." The Women's Canadian Historical Society of Toronto, *Transaction* 8 (1914).

Edgar, Matilda, ed. *Ten Years in Upper Canada*. Toronto: William Briggs, 1890.

Elizabeth Russell Papers, February 24, 1794. Metropolitan Toronto Library, Baldwin Room.

Elliott, James. *Billy Green and the Battle of Stoney Creek, June 6, 1813*. Stoney Creek, ON: Stoney Creek Historical Society, n.d.

Emerson, J.N., H.E. Devereux, and M.J. Ashworth. *A Study of Fort St. Joseph*. Ottawa: National Historic Parks and Sites Branch, Parks Canada, Department of Indian and Northern Affairs, 1977.

Farmer, Dennis, and Carol Farmer. *The King's Bread, 2nd Rising: Cooking at Niagara 1726–1815*. Youngstown, NY: Old Fort Niagara Association, 1989.

Firth, Edith. *The Town of York 1793–1815*. Toronto: University of Toronto Press/The Champlain Society, 1962.

FitzGibbon, Mary Agnes. "A Historic Banner: A Paper Read on February 8th, 1896." The Women's Canadian Historical Society of Toronto, *Transaction* 1 (n.d.).

Fort William: Hinge of a Nation. Toronto: National Heritage, 1970.

Franchère, Gabriel. *Narrative of a Voyage to the Northwest Coast of America*, 2nd ed. Chicago: Redfield, 1854.

Fryer, Mary Beacock. *Bold, Brave, and Born to Lead: Major General Isaac Brock and the Canadas.* Toronto: Dundurn Press, 2004.

Graham, M. Audrey. *150 Years at St. John's York Mills.* Toronto: General Publishing, 1966.

Graves, Donald E. *Red Coats & Grey Jackets: The Battle of Chippawa, 5 July 1814.* Toronto: Dundurn Press, 1994.

Gray, William. *Soldiers of the King: The Upper Canadian Militia 1812–1815.* Erin, ON: Boston Mills Press, 1995.

Great Britain, Treaties, Indian Treaties, and Surrenders. Ottawa, 1891.

Guillet, Edwin C. *Pioneer Settlement in Upper Canada.* Toronto: University of Toronto Press, 1969.

_____. *Pioneer Settlements.* Toronto: Ontario Publishing Company, 1933.

Hannon, Leslie F. *Forts of Canada: The Conflicts, Sieges, and Battles That Forged a Great Nation.* Toronto: McClelland & Stewart, 1969.

Harman, Daniel. *A Journal of Voyages and Travels in the Interior of North America.* Toronto: George N. Morang, 1904.

Hart, Patricia. *Pioneering in North York.* Toronto: General Publishing, 1968.

Henry, Alexander. *Travels and Adventures in Canada and the Indian Territories Between the Years 1760 and 1776.* New York, 1809.

Heron, Craig. *BOOZE: A Distilled History.* Toronto: Between the Lines, 2003.

Hicks, Elizabeth. *A True Romance of the American War of Independence 1775–1783.* London: William Hardwick, Peckham, 1903.

Higgins, W.H. *The Life and Times of Joseph Gould.* Toronto: C.B. Blackett Robinson, 1887.

Historical Glimpses of Lennox and Addington. Lennox and Addington County Council, 1964.

Hunter, Andrew F. *The History of Simcoe County*. Barrie, ON: Simcoe County Historical Society, 1909.

Innis, Mary Quayle, ed. *Mrs. Simcoe's Diary*. Toronto: Macmillan of Canada, 1965.

_____. *Mrs. Simcoe's Diary*. Toronto: Macmillan of Canada, 1971.

Jarvis, Hannah. *H. Jarvis Cookbook, and Health Remedies*, circa 1811.

Johnson, Leo A. *History of the County of Ontario 1615–1875*. Corporation of the County of Ontario, 1973.

Landmann, George Thomas. *Adventures and Recollections of Colonel Landmann*, vol. 1. London: Colburn and Co., 1852.

Lee, David. *The Fort on St. Joseph's Island*. Ottawa: National Historic Parks and Sites Branch, Parks Canada, Manuscript Report Series, No. 131, 1966.

Lefroy, Catherine F., ed. "Recollections of Mary Warren Breckenridge." The Women's Canadian Historical Society of Toronto, *Transaction* 3 (n.d.).

Life on the Farm. Ontario Ministry of Agriculture and Food, 1984.

Long, J. *Voyages and Travels of an Indian Interpreter and Trader*. London, 1791.

MacDonald, Margaret. *Whistler's Mother's Cook Book*. New York: George Putnam's Sons, 1979.

MacDonald, V.A. "Major-General Sir Isaac Brock." The Ontario Historical Society, *Papers and Records* 10 (1913).

Macfarlane, James. *The Cook Not Mad or Rational Cookery*. Kingston, Upper Canada, 1831.

Mallory, Enid L. *The Green Tiger: James FitzGibbon, A Hero of the War of 1812*. Toronto: McClelland & Stewart, 1976.

Martinello, I.L. *Call Us Canadians*. Toronto: McGraw-Hill Ryerson, 1976.

Marquis, G.G., ed. *Great Canadians*. Toronto, 1903.

McBurney, Margaret, and Mary Byers. *Tavern in the Town: Early Inns and Taverns in Ontario*. Toronto: University of Toronto Press, 1987.

McKay, John. *River Lake La Pluie Journal 1793–1794 and 1794–1795*. Hudson's Bay Archives, Microfilm B.105/a/5.

McNaught Frances, and Margaret Taylor. *The Early Canadian Galt Cook Book*. Toronto: William Briggs, 1898.

McPherson, Donald. *Fur Trade Journal, Lac La Pluie*. November 13, 1817.

Merritt, Richard, Nancy Butler, and Michael Power, eds. *The Capital Years: Niagara-on-the-Lake 1792–1796*. Toronto: Dundurn Press, 1991.

Nute, Grace Lee. *The Voyageur's Highway*. St. Paul, MN: Minnesota Historical Society, 1951.

Reaman, G.E. *The Trail of the Black Walnut*. Toronto: McClelland & Stewart, 1957.

Richardson, James. "Notes on Early Settlements." The Women's Canadian Historical Society of Toronto, *Annual Report and Transaction* 15 (1915–16).

Riddell, William Renwick. "Joseph Willcocks, Sheriff, Member of Parliament, and Traitor." The Ontario Historical Society, *Ontario History* 27 (1927).

_____. "Toronto in the Parliaments of Upper Canada, 1792–1841." The Women's Canadian Historical Society of Toronto, *Transaction* 22 (1921–22).

Robertson, J. Ross, ed. *The Diary of Mrs. John Graves Simcoe*. Toronto: William Briggs, 1911.

Robinson, Helen Caister. *Mistress Molly, the Brown Lady: A Portrait of Molly Brant*. Toronto: Dundurn Press, 1980.

Russell, Loris. "First Farms and the Development of Agriculture," in *Everyday Life in Nineteenth Century Ontario*. Toronto: Ontario Museum Association, 1978.

Seibel, George. *The Portage Road: 200 Years 1790–1990*. Niagara Falls, ON: City of Niagara Falls, 1990.

Sheppard, George. *Plunder, Profit, and Paroles: A Social History of the War of 1812 in Upper Canada*. Montreal and Kingston: McGill-Queen's University Press, 1994.

Simcoe County Pioneer Papers. Barrie, ON: Simcoe County Historical Society, 1908.

Smith, Michael. *A Geographical View of the Province of Upper Canada and Promiscuous Remarks on the Government*, 2nd ed. Trenton, ON: Moore & Lake, 1813.

Spragge, G.W. *The John Strachan Letterbook: 1812–1834*. Toronto: The Ontario Historical Society, 1946.

St-Denis, Guy. *Tecumseh's Bones*. Montreal and Kingston: McGill-Queen's University Press, 2005.

Stevenson, Matilda Coxe. "Ethnobotany of the Zuñi Indians." *Thirtieth Annual Report of the American Bureau of Ethnology to the Secretary of the Smithsonian Institution, 1908–1909*. Washington, DC: Government Printing Office, 1915.

Tasker, L.H. "The United Empire Loyalist Settlement at Long Point, Lake Erie." The Ontario Historical Society, *Papers and Records* 2 (1900).

Taylor, Alan. *The Civil War of 1812*. New York: Alfred A. Knopf, 2010.

Thompson, Mabel. "Billy Green the Scout." The Ontario Historical Society, *Ontario History* 4 (1952).

Tippet, William H. "The Hannah Ingraham Story." United Empire Loyalists' Association, *Annual Transactions* (1904–13).

Turner, Wesley B. *The War of 1812: The War That Both Sides Won*. 2nd ed. Toronto: Dundurn Press, 2000.

Wallace, W.S. "Fort William of the Fur Trade." *The Beaver* (December 1949).

Weeks, William. "The War of 1812: Civil Authority and Martial Law in Upper Canada," in *The Defended Border*, edited by Morris Zaslow. Toronto: Macmillan Company of Canada, 1964.

West, Bruce, "Dublin or Don," *Globe and Mail*, October 18, 1968.

Whisler, Frances L. *Indian Cookin'*. Nowega Press, 1973.

Williams, Jack. *Merritt: A Canadian Before His Time*. St. Catharines, ON: Stonehouse Publications, 1985.

Wood, William R. *Past Years in Pickering: Sketches of the History of the Community*. Toronto: William Briggs, 1911.

Young, A.H. "Letters from the Secretary of Upper Canada and Mrs. Jarvis to Her Father, the Reverend Samuel Peters, DD." The Women's Canadian Historical Society of Toronto, *Annual Report and Transaction* 23 (1922–23).

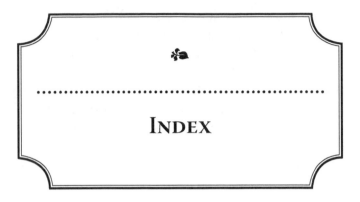

INDEX